I0192563

Two Views
of
Shiloh

Two Views
of
Shiloh

"Shiloh" as Seen by a Private Soldier
Warren Olney

The Battle of Shiloh
Joseph W. Rich

LEONAUR

Two Views
of
Shiloh
"Shiloh" as Seen by a Private Soldier by Warren Olney
The Battle of Shiloh by Joseph W. Rich

First published under the titles
"Shiloh" as Seen by a Private Soldier
and
The Battle of Shiloh

Leonaur is an imprint of Oakpast Ltd

Copyright in this form © 2009 Oakpast Ltd

ISBN: 978-1-84677-892-6 (hardcover)
ISBN: 978-1-84677-891-9 (softcover)

http://www.leonaur.com

Publisher's Notes

In the interests of authenticity, the spellings, grammar and place names used have been retained from the original editions.

The opinions of the authors represent a view of events in which he was a participant related from his own perspective, as such the text is relevant as an historical document.

The views expressed in this book are not necessarily those of the publisher.

Contents

"Shiloh" as Seen by a Private Soldier

Warren Olney

Contents

The Battle of Shiloh
WITH SOME PERSONAL REMINISCENCES

Very interesting descriptions of the great battles of the late war, written by prominent generals, have been lately published and widely read. It seems to me, however, that it is time for the private soldier to be heard from.

Of course, his field of vision is much more limited than that of his general. On the other hand, it is of vital importance to the latter to gloss over his mistakes, and draw attention only to those things which will add to his reputation. The private soldier has no such feeling. It is only to the officers of high rank engaged that a battle can bring glory and renown. To the army of common soldiers, who do the actual fighting, and risk mutilation and death, there is no reward except the consciousness of duty bravely performed. This was peculiarly the case in the late war, when more than a million of young men, the flower of our country, left their workshops and farms, their schools and colleges, to endure the hardships of the march and the camp, to risk health, limb and life, that their country might live, expecting nothing, hoping nothing for themselves, but all for their fatherland.

The first really great battle of the war was that of Pittsburg Landing, or Shiloh, and I shall not only attempt to give a general account of the battle, but also describe it from the point of view of a man in the ranks.

In respect to the general features of this desperate struggle between our own countrymen, my statements are derived from many reports and accounts carefully collated, and from many conversations with soldiers engaged, both from the Union and Confederate armies.

Who of us, having reached middle life, does not recall the exultation and enthusiasm aroused by the news of the capture of Fort Donelson? What a thrill of pride and patriotism was felt through all the loyal North! The soldiers of the great Northwest had attacked a citadel of the rebellion, and captured it, with sixteen thousand of its defenders.

At this time the Third Iowa Infantry was strung along the North Missouri Railroad, guarding bridges and doing other police work. Company B, which had the honour of having on its muster roll private Olney, was stationed at that time in the little town of Sturgeon, Missouri, where our principal occupation was to keep from freezing. We had then spent eight months campaigning in that border State—that is, if you call guarding railways and bridges, and attempting to overawe the disaffected, enlivened now and then by a brisk skirmish, campaigning. The Second Iowa had led the charge which captured the hostile breastworks at Donelson, and General Grant had telegraphed to General Halleck at St. Louis, who had repeated the message to the Governor of our State, that the Second Iowa was the bravest of the brave. The First Iowa had distinguished itself at Wilson's Creek, near Springfield, under General Lyon, while *we*—well, we hadn't done much of anything but to get a licking at Blue Mills. Therefore, when a message to move came, and we found ourselves on the way to join General Grant's army, we felt quite hilarious.

At St. Louis we were put on board the steamer *Iatan*. Down the Mississippi, up the Ohio, up the Tennessee. As we proceeded up the Tennessee we were continually overtaking or being joined by other steamboats loaded with troops, until presently the river was alive with transports, carrying the army of the West right into the heart of the Confederacy. It was a beautiful and stirring sight; mild weather had set in (it was now the second week of March), the flotilla of steamboats, black with soldiers, bands playing, flags flying, all combined to arouse and interest. It was the "pomp and circumstance of glorious war."

Frequent stoppages were made, giving us a chance to run ashore. About the thirteenth we reached the landing-place, which soon afterwards became famous. The river was very high, and at first there seemed to be doubts as to where a landing should be effected, but in a few days the question was settled. Our boat was moored as near the shore as possible, and we joined the immense throng painfully making their way through the unfathomable mud to camps in the dense woods. The first things I observed after reaching the high bluff, were trees that had been torn and shattered by shells from our gunboats, which, it seems, had dislodged a company of Confederates, who had dug rifle-pits on the bluff, from whence they had fired on our steamboats.

We first camped on the bluff near the landing, but shortly moved back about a mile from the river, and camped on the edge of a small cotton field with dense forests all around. The Hamburg road ran past the left of our line, between us and the Forty-first Illinois; while on the right was a small ravine, which ran into a little creek, and that into Snake Creek.

The mud—well, it was indescribable. Though we were only a mile from our base of supplies, the greatest difficulty was experienced in getting camp equipage and provisions. We found that other divisions of the army had landed before us, moving farther out to the front towards Corinth, and had so cut up the roads that they were quagmires their whole length. Teams were stalled in the mud in every direction. The principal features of the landscape were trees, mud, wagons buried to the hub, and struggling, plunging mule teams. The shouts of teamsters and resounding whacks filled the air; and as to profanity- well, you could see the air about an enraged teamster turn blue as he exhorted his impenitent mules. And the rain! how it did come down! As I recall it, the spring of 1862 did not measure its rainfall in Western Tennessee by inches, but by feet.

But in time our camp was fairly established. Sibley tents were distributed, one for fourteen men. They protected us from the rain, but they had their drawbacks. Several of us were schoolmates from a Western college, and, of course, in some respects, constituted a little aristocracy. We had had a small tent to ourselves, and the socialistic grayback, as yet, had not crawled therein. Now, we were required to share our tent with others, and that might mean a great many. But when it came to a question of sleeping out in the cold rain, or camping down in a crowded tent in true democratic equality and taking the chances of immigration from our neighbours' clothing, we did not prefer the rain.

Of course, the private soldier has not much opportunity for exploration about his camp, however strong may be his passion in that direction. I did what I could, but my knowledge of the general encampment was much enlarged when, during the days following the battle, all discipline being relaxed, I tramped the field over in every direction and talked with the men of numerous regiments on their camp grounds. Further on, I shall refer to the position occupied by our army more at length, and shall only refer now to the general position of our encampment, as on a wooded plateau, accessible to attack only from the direction of Corinth, the river being in our rear, Snake Creek and Owl Creek on our right flank, and Lick Creek on our left.

In places there were small fields with their adjuncts of deserted cabins. Our troops were camped wherever there was an opening in the woods or underbrush sufficiently large for a regiment. There seemed to be no order or system about the method of encampment, but each regiment occupied such suitable ground as presented itself in the neighbourhood of the rest of the brigade; and the same was true of the brigades composing the divisions.

Our regiment was brigaded with the Twenty-eighth, Thirty-second, and Forty-first Illinois. The division was commanded by Brigadier-General Stephen A. Hurlbut (since somewhat noted as United States Minister to Peru). We had served under him in Missouri, and our principal recollection of him was an event which occurred at Macon. We had got aboard a train of cattle cars for the purpose of going to the relief of some point threatened by the enemy. After waiting on the train two or three hours, expecting every moment to start, we noticed a couple of staff officers supporting on each side the commanding general, and leading him to the car I was in. Getting him to the side of the car, they boosted him in at the door, procured a soldier's knapsack for him to sit on, and left him. He was so drunk he couldn't sit upright. The consequence was that the regimental officers refused to move. A court-martial followed, and we heard no more of our general until we found him at Pittsburg Landing in command of a division. He showed so much coolness and bravery in the battle which followed, that we forgave him his first scandalous appearance. But the distrust of him before the battle can readily be imagined.

No one who has not been through the experience can realize the anxiety of the private soldier respecting the character and capacity of his commanding officer. His life is in the general's hand. Whether he shall be uselessly sacrificed, may depend wholly upon the coolness or readiness for an emergency of the commander; whether he has had two drinks or three; whether he has had a good night's rest, or a good cigar. The private soldier regards a new and unknown commander very much as a slave does a new owner, and with good reason. Without confidence on the part of the rank and file, victory is impossible. Their soldiers' confidence in Stonewall Jackson and Lee doubled the effective strength of their armies. When in the Franco-Prussian war a German regiment was called upon for a charge, each man felt that the order was given because it was necessary, and that what he was doing was part of a comprehensive scheme, whose success might very likely depend upon whether he did his assigned part manfully. The French soldier in that war had no such feeling and, of course, the result of that campaign was not long in doubt.

In Napoleon's time, the confidence of the rank and file was such that time and again he was saved from defeat by the feeling of the attacked corps or detachment that it *must* hold its ground, or probably imperil the army. Oh, the sickening doubt and distrust of our generals during the first years of the war! Our soldiers were as brave as ever trod the earth, and thoroughly imbued with the cause for which they were fighting; but the suspicion that at headquarters there might be inefficiency or drunkenness; that marches and counter-marches had no definite purpose; that their lives might be uselessly thrown away— you would have to go through it to realize it! At the beginning of the war, the Southerners had a vast advantage over us in that respect. Generally speaking, they started out with the same able commanders they had at the end.

Our colonel was thoroughly disliked and distrusted. As he was the ranking colonel of the brigade, he was placed in command of it; so you see we did not feel particularly happy over the situation, especially as we knew the Confederate army was only twenty-two miles off.

The steady, cold rains of the first week or two was most depressing. On account, probably, of the bad weather and exposure, the soldiers' worst enemy, diarrhoea, took possession of our camps, and for a week or ten days we literally had no stomachs for fighting. But after a little the rain let up, the sun came out warm, our spirits revived, the roads, and consequently the supplies improved; and on the whole, we thought it rather jolly.

If you had been there of a warm, sunny day you would have noticed every log and stump serving as a seat for a soldier, who had taken off his shirt and was diligently hunting it all over. It was not safe to ask him what he was looking for.

Troops were continually arriving, some of them freshly recruited, and not yet familiar with their arms, or the simplest elements of regimental manoeuvres. It was said there were some regiments who had just received their guns, and had never fired them. Badeau says they came on the field without cartridges. I know that improved rifles were scarce, for my own regiment at that time did not have rifles, but old smooth bore muskets with buck-and-ball ammunition—that is, the cartridge had next to the powder a large ball, and then next to it three buck shot. Of course, we should have had no show against rifles at long range, but at short range, in woods and brush, these weapons were fearfully destructive, as we shall presently see.

Strange to say, these freshly recruited regiments were assigned to Sherman's division and to Prentiss' division, whose camps were scattered in the woods farthest out towards Corinth. As might have been expected, these new soldiers did not stand on the order of their going, when they suddenly discovered a hostile army on top of them.

A map of the place selected for the concentration of our army shows that with proper precautions and such defensive works as, later in the war, would have been constructed within a few hours, the place was impregnable. The river which ran in the rear was controlled by our gunboats, and furnished us the means of obtaining abundant supplies. Creeks with marshy banks protected either flank. The only possible avenue of attack upon this position was directly in front, and across that ran little creeks and ravines, with here and there open fields affording fine vantage-ground. A general anticipating the possibility of attack, would not have scattered his divisions so widely, and would have marked a line of defence upon which the troops should rally.

Advantage would have been taken of the ground, and trees felled with the tops outwards, through which an attacking force would have, with great difficulty, to struggle. And later in the war, as a matter of precaution, and because of the proximity of the enemy, breastworks would have been thrown up. All this could have been done in a few hours. Our flanks were so well protected that no troops were needed there, and in case of attack, each division commander should have had his place in the front, to which to immediately march his command; while, the line being not more than three miles long at the very outside estimate, there were abundant forces to man it thoroughly, leaving a large force in the reserve to reinforce a point imperilled.

Why was not this done? It is hard to find an answer. General Sherman's division was at the extreme front. It was being organized. The enemy was not more than twenty-two miles away, and was known to be concentrating from all the West. Yet this general, who afterwards acquired such fame as a consummate master of the art of war, took no precautions whatever, not even thoroughly scouting the ground in his front. His pickets could not have been out more than a mile. General Prentiss' division was also in process of organization, and he, like Sherman, was in advance, and on Sherman's left. The complete absence of the ordinary precautions, always taken by military commanders since the beginning of history, is inexplicable.

The only reason I can conjecture for it grows out of the character of General Grant and his distinguished subordinate, and their inexperience. They had had then little practical knowledge of actual warfare. General Sherman, except on one occasion, had never heard a hostile gun fired. They had to learn their art, and the country and their army had to pay the cost of their teaching. Happily, they were able to profit by every lesson, and soon had no equals among our commanders. But because they have since deserved so well of their country, is no reason why history should be silent as to their mistakes. The Confederates would have made a great mistake in attacking us at all in such a position, if we had been prepared to receive them. But this want of preparation prevented us from taking advantage of the opportunity, and inflicting a crushing defeat upon the South. By it the war was prolonged, and every village and hamlet in the West had its house of mourning.

Immediately in the right rear of General Sherman was camped the veteran division of General McClernand. About two miles further back, and about a mile from the river, was stationed the reserve, consisting of two divisions, Hurlbut's and W. H. L. Wallace's, formerly C. F. Smith's. Across Owl Creek, and seven or eight miles off, was camped General Lew Wallace's division. It was so far away as not to be in easy supporting distance.

On April 1st, our division was marched to an open field, and there carefully reviewed by General Grant. This was our first sight of the victor of Donelson. Friday, the 4th of April, was a sloppy day, and just before sundown we heard firing off towards Sherman's division. We fell into line and started toward the front. After we had marched about a mile, pitch darkness came on. Presently, a staff officer directed a counter-march back to camp, saying it was only a rebel reconnoisance. It was a nasty march back in the mud, dense woods, and thick darkness.

All this day the Confederate army was struggling through the woods and mud, on its march from Corinth to attack us. It was the expectation of General Johnston and his subordinates to cover the intervening space between the two armies in this one day and attack early Saturday morning; but the difficulties of the march was such, that he did not make more than half the distance, and had to go into camp for the night. Saturday was a reasonably pleasant day, but General Johnston's troops had got so entangled in the forests, he did not feel justified in attacking until all his preparations were made, which took the whole of Saturday. He then moved up to within a mile or two of Sherman and Prentiss, and went into camp *within sound of our drums*.

The delay had been so great that Beauregard now advised a countermarch back to Corinth. He represented that our forces had surely been appraised of their march, and it would be too late now to effect a surprise; that they would undoubtedly find us all prepared, and probably behind breastworks and other obstructions. General Johnston was smarting under the criticisms of the campaign which resulted in the loss of Donelson. His courage and military instinct told him that now was the time to strike. He felt, too, that a bold stroke was necessary to redeem the fortunes of the Confederacy and his own reputation. His resolution was to conquer or die; and he replied to Beauregard: "We shall attack at daylight tomorrow."

Here was an army of a little over 40,000 men, as brave as ever shouldered muskets, fighting on their own soil, and, as they believed, for homes and liberty, resting for the night at about two miles from the invading army, and all prepared to attack at dawn, and sweep the invaders of their country back into the Tennessee River. Upon the favouring breeze, the sound of our drums at evening parade came floating to their ears. They heard the bugle note enjoying quiet and repose in the camp of their unsuspecting foe. They, themselves, were crouching in the thick woods and darkness, all prepared to spring on their prey. No camp-fire was lighted; no unnecessary sound was permitted; but silent, watchful, with mind and heart prepared for conflict, the Southern hosts waited for the morning.

Such was the situation, so far as our enemies were concerned. But how was it with the army fighting for the integrity and preservation of the nation? Let us begin with the commanding General. That day (Saturday) he dispatched General Halleck as follows:

"The main force of the army is at Corinth. . . The number at Corinth and within supporting distance of it cannot be far from 80,000 men." Later in the day he dispatched the news of the enemy's reconnoisance the night before, and added: "I have scarcely the faintest idea of an attack (general one) being made upon us, but will be prepared should a thing take place."

Grant had less than 50,000 men fit for battle. He thinks the enemy at Corinth, twenty-two miles away, has 80,000 men. He must know that the enemy knows Buell, with his army, will soon reach the Tennessee, and when united with his own will nearly double his effective strength; that now, and before Buell joins him, if ever, must the Confederates strike an effective blow. His pickets have been driven in the night before, the enemy using a piece or two of artillery; yet he does not expect an attack, and makes not the slightest preparation to receive or repel one. He leaves General Lew Wallace with over 7,000 good troops at Crump's Landing, out of easy supporting distance, Nelson's division and Crittenden's division of Buell's army at Savannah; and has no thought of moving them up that day to repel an overwhelming attack about to be made on him. On Saturday he visits his army and Sherman, and then goes back to Savannah, unsuspicious of the presence of the enemy.

How was it with General Sherman, who had the advance on the right, and was probably more relied upon by Grant and Halleck than was Prentiss? In fact it is not at all improbable that Grant wholly relied upon the two division commanders at the front, particularly Sherman, to keep him posted as to the movements of the hostile army. General Sherman reported on Saturday that he thought there were about two regiments of infantry and a battery of artillery about six miles out. As a matter of fact, the whole rebel army was not more than six miles out. Later in the day he dispatches: "The enemy is saucy, but got the worst of it yesterday, and will not press our pickets far. I do not apprehend anything like an attack on our position."

A tolerably extensive reading of campaigns and military histories justifies me in saying that such an exhibition of unsuspicious security in the presence of a hostile army is without a parallel in the history of warfare.

How was it with our army? We knew the enemy to be at Corinth, but there had been no intimation of advance; and no army could get over the intervening space in less than two days, of which, of course, it was the duty of our generals to have ample notice. Usually, before a battle, there seems to be something in the very air that warns the soldier and officer of what is coming, and to nerve themselves for the struggle; but most of us retired this Saturday night to our blankets in as perfect fancied security as ever enveloped an army.

But this was not true of all. A sense of uneasiness pervaded a portion of the advance line. Possibly there had been too much noise in the woods in front, possibly that occult sense, which tells us of the proximity of another, warned them of the near approach of a hostile army. Some of the officers noticed that the woods beyond the pickets seemed to be full of Rebel cavalry. General Prentiss was infected with this uneasiness, and at daylight on Sunday morning sent out the Twenty-first Missouri to make an observation towards Corinth.

This regiment, proceeding through the forest, ran plump upon the Confederate skirmish line, which it promptly attacked. Immediately the Missourians saw an army behind the skirmish line advancing upon them. They could hold their ground but for a moment. The enemy's advance swept them back, and, like an avalanche, the Confederate army poured into the camps of Sherman's and Prentiss' divisions.

At the first fire our men sprang to arms. By the time the enemy had reached our camps many regiments had become partially formed, but they were all unnerved by the shock. Some were captured by the enemy before they could get their clothes on. Some, without firing a shot, broke for the river-landing, three miles away, and cowered beneath its banks. General Sherman and his staff mounted their horses, and as they galloped past the Fifty-third Ohio, which was getting into line, one of the officers called out to him not to go any farther, for the rebel army was just beyond the rising ground. The general made use of some expression about not getting frightened at a reconnoisance, and went ahead. As he reached the slight elevation he beheld the Confederate army sweeping down upon him.

Their skirmish line fired at him, killing his orderly. He realized at last that he was in the presence of a hostile army. From that moment he did everything that mortal man could do to retrieve his fatal mistake. Wounded twice, several horses successively killed under him, chaos and defeat all around, yet his clear intelligence and steady courage stamped him a born leader of men. The other generals and officers yielded to his superior force and obeyed his orders. He was everywhere, encouraging, threatening, organizing, and succeeded in establishing a tolerable line in the rear of his camps.

General Prentiss' troops were more demoralized than Sherman's. Whole regiments broke away, and were not reorganized until after the battle. A tide of fugitives set in toward the landing, carrying demoralization and terror with them.

Our camp was so far back that we heard nothing of this early uproar. The morning was a beautiful one, and after our early breakfast I started down the little creek, hunting for some first flowers of spring. I had scarcely got out of sight of camp, when the firing toward the front, though faintly heard, seemed too steady to be caused by the pernicious habit which prevailed of the pickets firing off their guns on returning from duty, preparatory to cleaning them. A sense of apprehension took possession of me. Presently artillery was heard, and then I turned toward camp, getting more alarmed at every step.

When I reached camp a startled look was on every countenance. The musketry firing had become loud and general, and whole batteries of artillery were joining in the dreadful chorus. The men rushed to their tents and seized their guns, but as yet no order to fall in was given. Nearer and nearer sounded the din of a tremendous conflict. Presently the long roll was heard from the regiments on our right. A staff officer came galloping up, spoke a word to the Major in command, the order to fall in was shouted, the drummers began to beat the long roll, and it was taken up by the regiments on our left. The men, with pale faces, wild eyes, compressed lips, quickly accoutred themselves for battle.

The shouts of the officers, the rolling of the drums, the hurrying to and fro of the men, the uproar of approaching but unexpected battle, all together produced sensations which cannot be described. Soon, teams with shouting drivers came tearing along the road toward the landing. Crowds of fugitives and men slightly wounded went hurrying past in the same direction. Uproar and turmoil were all around; but we, having got into line, stood quietly with scarcely a word spoken. Each man was struggling with himself and nerving himself for what bid fair to be a dreadful conflict. What thoughts of home and kindred and all that makes life dear come to one at such a moment.

Presently a staff officer rode up, the command to march was given, and with the movement came some relief to the mental and moral strain. As we passed in front of the Forty-first Illinois, a field officer of that regiment, in a clear, ringing voice, was speaking to his men, and announced that if any man left the ranks on pretence of caring for the wounded he should be shot on the spot; that the wounded must be left till the fight was over. His men cheered him, and we took up the cheer. Blood was beginning to flow through our veins again, and we could even comment to one another upon the sneaks who remained in camp, on pretence of being sick.

As we moved toward the front the fugitives and the wounded increased in numbers. Poor wretches, horribly mutilated, would drop down, unable to go farther. Wagons full of wounded, filling the air with their groans, went hurrying by. As we approached the scene of conflict, we moved off to the left of the line of the rear-ward going crowd, crossed a small field and halted in the open woods beyond.

As we halted, we saw right in front of us, but about three hundred or four hundred yards off, a dense line of Confederate infantry, quietly standing in ranks. In our excitement, and without a word of command, we turned loose and with our smooth bore muskets opened fire upon them. After three or four rounds, the absurdity of firing at the enemy at that distance with our guns dawned upon us, and we stopped. As the smoke cleared up we saw the enemy still there, not having budged or fired a shot in return. But though our action was absurd, it was a relief to us to do something, and we were rapidly becoming toned up to the point of steady endurance.

As we gazed at the enemy so coolly standing there, an Ohio battery of artillery came galloping up in our rear, and what followed I don't believe was equalled by anything of the kind during the war. As the artillery came up we moved off by the right flank a few steps, to let it come in between us and the Illinois regiment next on our left. Where we were standing was in open, low-limbed oak timber. The line of Southern infantry was in tolerably plain view through the openings in the woods, and were still standing quietly. Of course, we all turned our heads away from them to look at the finely equipped battery, as it came galloping from the rear to our left flank, its officers shouting directions to the riders where to stop their guns.

It was the work of but an instant to bring every gun into position. Like a flash the gunners leaped from their seats and unlimbered the cannon. The fine six-horse teams began turning round with the caissons, charges were being rammed home, and the guns pointed toward the dense ranks of the enemy, when, from right in front, a dense puff of smoke, a tearing of shot and shell through the trees, a roar from half a dozen cannon, hitherto unseen, and our brave battery was knocked into smithereens. Great limbs of trees, torn off by cannon shot, came down on horse and rider, crushing them to earth. Shot and shell struck cannon, upsetting them; caissons exploded them. Not a shot was fired from our side.

But how those astounded artillery men—those of them who could run at all—did scamper out of there. Like Mark Twain's dog, they may be running yet. At least, it is certain that no attempt was ever made to reorganize that battery—it was literally wiped out then and there.

This made us feel mightily uncomfortable—in fact, we had been feeling quite uncomfortable all the morning. It did not particularly add to the cheerfulness of the prospect, to reflect that our division was the reserve of the army, and should not be called into action, ordinarily, until towards the close of the battle; while here we were, early in the forenoon, face to face with the enemy, our battery of artillery gobbled up at one mouthful, and the rest of the army in great strait, certainly, and probably demoralized.

One of the cannon shot had gone through our colonel's horse, and the rider had been carried off the field. Colonel Pugh, of the Forty-first Illinois, then took command of the brigade, about-faced us, and marched us back across the little field, and halted us just behind the fence, the enemy during this manoeuvre leaving us wholly undisturbed.

The rails were thrown down and we lay flat upon the ground, while another battery came up and opened on the enemy, who had moved up almost to the wreck of our first battery.

Here, then, began a fierce artillery duel. Shot and shell went over us and crashing through the trees to the rear of us, and I suppose that shot and shell went crashing through the trees above the enemy; but if they didn't suffer any more from shot and shell than we did, there was a great waste of powder and iron that day. But how a fellow does hug the ground under such circumstances! As a shell goes whistling over him he flattens out, and presses himself into the earth, almost. Pity the sorrows of a big fat man under such a fire.

Later in the war we should have dug holes for ourselves with bayonets. We must have lain there hugging the ground for more than two hours, with now and then an intermission, listening to the flight of dreaded missiles above us; but, as nobody in our immediate neighbourhood was hurt, we at length voted the performance of the artillery to be, on the whole, rather fine. During intermissions, while the scenes were shifting, as it were, we began to feel a disposition to talk and joke over the situation.

The reason why we were not subjected to an infantry fire, was because the enemy's forces, tangled in the wooded country, and in places beaten back by the stubborn gallantry of our surprised but not demoralized men, needed to be reorganized. All the Southern accounts agree that their brigades and divisions had become mixed in apparently hopeless confusion. The battlefield was so extensive that fighting was going on at some point all the time, so that at no time was there a complete cessation of the roar of artillery or the rattle of musketry.

Two or three times General Hurlbut came riding along our line; and once, during a lull, General Grant and staff came slowly riding by, the General with a cigar in his mouth, and apparently as cool and unconcerned as if inspection was the sole purpose of visiting us. The General's apparent indifference had, undoubtedly, a good influence on the men. They saw him undisturbed, and felt assured that the worst was over, and the attack had spent its force.

This must have been soon after he reached the field; for, upon hearing the roar of battle in the morning at Savannah he went aboard a steamer, came up the river eight or nine miles, and did not reach the scene of action much, if any, before 10 o'clock. By that time, Sherman, McClernand and Prentiss had been driven more than a mile beyond their camps, and with such of their command as they could hold together had formed on the flanks of the two reserve divisions of Hurlbut and W. H. L. Wallace, who had moved forward beyond their own camps to meet them.

While General Johnston and his adjutants were reorganizing their command after their first great triumph, to complete the conquest so well begun, Grant and his generals were attempting to organize resistance out of defeat, to establish their lines, to connect the divisions with each other, and improve the situation of the different commands by seizing the most favourable ground. Sherman and McClernand, with what remained of their divisions, were on the extreme right; W. H. L. Wallace, whose division had not yet come into action, on their left, and on the left centre of our army; Prentiss on his left. Then came Hurlbut; then a small force under Stuart, on the extreme left of our line.

Fortunately for us, General Johnston's plan was to attack our left. If, when he was ready to renew the battle, he had assailed our right, where were Sherman's and McClernand's divisions, who had already done almost as much as flesh and blood could stand, nothing would have stopped him, and by two o'clock we should have been where we were at dark—that is, huddled about the landing. Then there would have been nothing to do but to surrender. Happily, most happily, when he renewed the assaults upon our lines, it was upon those portions manned by reserve divisions, troops that had not been seriously engaged, and had had time to steady their nerves, and to select favourable positions.

As for myself and comrades, we had become accustomed to the situation somewhat. The lull in the fighting in our immediate vicinity, and the reports which reached us that matters were now progressing favourably on the rest of the field, reassured us. We were becoming quite easy in mind. I had always made it a rule to keep a supply of sugar and some hard tack in my haversack, ready for an emergency. It stood me in good stead just then, for I alone had something besides fighting for lunch. I nibbled my hard tack, and ate my sugar with comfort and satisfaction, for I don't believe three men of our regiment were hurt by this artillery fire upon us, which had been kept up with more or less fury for two or three hours.

One of the little episodes of the battle happened about this time. We noticed that a Confederate, seated on one of the abandoned cannon I have mentioned, was leisurely taking an observation. He was out of range of our guns, but our First Lieutenant got a rifle from a man who happened to have one, took deliberate aim, and Johnny Reb tumbled.

But soon after noon the Confederate forces were ready to hurl themselves on our lines. There had been more or less fighting on our right all the time, but now Johnston had collected his troops and massed them in front of the Union army's left. Language is inadequate to give an idea of the situation. Cannon and musketry roared and rattled, not in volleys, but in one continual din. Charge after charge was made upon the Union lines, and every time repulsed. By concentrating the main body of his troops on our left, General Johnston was superior there to us in numbers, and there was no one upon whom we could call for help. General Lew Wallace had not taken the precaution to learn the roads between his division at Crump's Landing and the main body, and he and his 7,000 men were lost in the woods, instead of being where they could support us in this our dire extremity.

The left wing of our brigade was the Hornet's Nest, mentioned in the Southern accounts of the battle. On the immediate right of my regiment was timber with growth of underbrush, and the dreadful conflict set the woods on fire, burning the dead and the wounded who could not crawl away. At one point not burned over, I noticed, after the battle, a strip of low underbrush which had evidently been the scene of a most desperate contest. Large patches of brush had been cut off by bullets at about as high as a man's waist, as if mowed with a scythe, and I could not find in the whole thicket a bush which had not at some part of it been touched by a ball. Of course, human beings could not exist in such a scene, save by closely hugging the ground, or screening themselves behind trees.

Hour after hour passed. Time and again the Confederate hordes threw themselves on our lines, and were repulsed; but our ranks were becoming dangerously thinned. If a few thousand troops could have been brought from Lew Wallace's division to our sorely-tried left the battle would have been won. His failure to reach us was fatal.

Yet, during all this terrible ordeal through which our comrades on the immediate right and the left of us were passing, we were left undisturbed until about two o'clock. Then there came from the woods on the other side of the field, to the edge of it, and then came trotting across it, as fine looking a body of men as I ever expect to see under arms. They came with their guns at what soldiers call right shoulder shift. Lying on the ground there, with the rails of the fence thrown down in front of us, we beheld them, as they started in beautiful line; then increasing their speed as they neared our side of the field, they came on till they reached the range of our smooth bore guns, loaded with buck and ball. Then we rose with a volley right in their faces.

Of course, the smoke then entirely obscured the vision, but with eager, bloodthirsty energy, we loaded and fired our muskets at the top of our speed, aiming low, until, from not noticing any return fire, the word passed along from man to man to stop firing. As the smoke rose so that we could see over the field, that splendid body of men presented to my eyes more the appearance of a wind-row of hay than anything else. They seemed to be piled up on each other in a long row across the field. Probably the obscurity caused by the smoke, as well as the slight slope of the ground towards us, accounted for this piled up appearance, for it was something which could not possibly occur. But the slaughter had been fearful.

Here and there you could see a squad of men running off out of range; now and then a man lying down, probably wounded or stunned, would rise and try to run, soon to tumble from the shots we sent after him. After the action I went all over the field of battle, visiting every part of it; but in no place was there anything like the number of dead upon the same space of ground as here in this little field. Our old fashioned guns, loaded as they were, and at such close quarters, had done fearful execution. This is undoubtedly the same field General Grant speaks of in the Century article, but he is mistaken when he speaks of the dead being from both sides. There were no Union dead in that field.

Our casualties were small. In our little set of college boys only one, was hurt; he receiving a wound in the leg, which caused its amputation. The bayonet of my gun was shot off, but possibly that was done by some man behind me, firing just as I threw the muzzle of my gun into his way. I didn't notice it until, in loading my gun, I struck my hand against the jagged end of the broken piece.

The Confederates had all they wanted of charging across the field, and let us alone. But just to our left General Johnston had personally organized and started a heavy assaulting column. Overwhelmed by numbers, the Forty-first and Thirty-second Illinois gave way from the position they had so tenaciously held, but one of their last shots mortally wounded the Confederate general. The gallant Lieutenant-Colonel of the Forty-first, whom we had cheered as we moved out in the morning, was killed, and his regiment, broken and cut to pieces, did not renew the fight.

Making that break in our line, after four or five hours of as hard fighting as ever occurred on this continent, was the turning point of the day. American had met American in fair, stand-up fight, and our side was beaten, because we could not reinforce the point which was assailed by the concentrated forces of the enemy.

Of course, the giving way on our left necessitated our abandoning the side of the field from whence we had annihilated an assaulting column. We moved back a short distance in the woods, and a crowd of our enemies promptly occupied the position we had left. Then began the first real, prolonged fighting experienced by our regiment that day. Our success in crushing the first attack had exhilarated us. We had tasted blood and were thoroughly aroused.

Screening ourselves behind every log and tree, all broken into squads, the enemy broken up likewise, we gave back shot for shot and yell for yell. The very madness of bloodthirstiness possessed us. To kill, to exterminate the beings in front of us was our whole desire. Such energy and force was too much for our enemies, and ere long we saw squads of them rising from the ground and running away. Again there was no foe in our front. Ammunition was getting short, but happily a wagon came up with cartridges, and we took advantage of the lull to fill our boxes. We had not yet lost many men and were full of fight.

This contest exploded all my notions derived from histories and pictures, of the way men stand up in the presence of the enemy. Unless in making an assault or moving forward, both sides hugged the ground as closely as they possibly could and still handle their guns. I doubt if a human being could have existed three minutes, if standing erect in open ground under such a fire as we here experienced. As for myself, at the beginning I jumped behind a little sapling not more than six inches in diameter, and instantly about six men ranged themselves behind me, one behind the other. I thought they would certainly shoot my ears off, and I would be in luck if the side of my head didn't go. The reports of their guns were deafening. A savage remonstrance was unheeded. I was behind a sapling and proposed to stay there. They were behind me and proposed to stay there.

The sapling did me a good turn, small as it was. It caught some Rebel bullets, as I ascertained for a certainty afterwards. I fancied at the time that I heard the spat of the bullets as they struck.

Here my particular chum was wounded by a spent ball, and crawled off the field. I can see him yet, writhing at my feet, grasping the leaves and sticks in the horrible pain which the blow from a spent ball inflicts. A bullet struck the top of the forehead of the wit of the company, plowing along the skull without breaking it. His dazed expression, as he turned instinctively to crawl to the rear, was so comical as to cause a laugh even there.

The lull caused by the death of General Johnston did not last long, and again on our left flank great masses of the enemy appeared, and we had to fall back two or three hundred yards.

Then began another fight. But this time the odds were overwhelmingly against us. At it we went, but in front and quartering on the left thick masses of the enemy slowly but steadily advanced upon us. This time it was a log I got behind, kneeling, loading and firing into the dense ranks of the enemy advancing right in front, eager to kill, kill! I lost thought of companions, until a ball struck me fair in the side, just under the arm, knocking me over. I felt it go clear through my body, struggled on the ground with the effect of the blow for an instant, recovered myself, sprang to my feet, saw I was alone, my comrades already on the run, the enemy close in on the left as well as front—saw it all at a glance, felt I was mortally wounded, and—took to my heels.

Run! such time was never made before; overhauled my companions in no time; passed them; began to wonder that a man shot through the body could run so fast, and to suspect that perhaps I was not mortally wounded after all; felt for the hole the ball had made, found it in the blouse and shirt, bad bruise on the ribs, nothing more—spent ball; never relaxed my speed; saw everything around—see it yet. I see the enemy close in on the flank, pouring in their fire at short range. I see our men running for their lives, men every instant tumbling forward limp on their faces, men falling wounded and rolling on the ground, the falling bullets raising little puffs of dust on apparently every foot of ground, a bullet through my hair, a bullet through my trousers. I hear the cruel *iz, iz,* of the minie balls everywhere. Ahead I see artillery galloping for the landing, and crowds of men running with almost equal speed, and all in the same direction. I even see the purple tinge given by the setting sun to the dust and smoke of battle. I see unutterable defeat, the success of the rebellion, a great catastrophe, a moral and physical cataclysm.

No doubt, in less time than it takes to recall these impressions, we ran out of this horrible gauntlet—a party who shall be nameless still in the lead of the regiment.

Before getting out of it we crossed our camp ground, and here one of our college set, the captain of the company fell, with several holes through his body, while two others of our set were wounded. In that short race at least one-third of our little command were stricken down.

Immediately behind us the Confederates closed in, and the brave General Prentiss and the gallant remains of his command were cut off and surrendered. As we passed out of range of the enemy's fire we mingled with the masses of troops skurrying towards the landing, all semblance of organization lost. It was a great crowd of beaten troops. Pell-mell we rushed towards the landing. As we approached it we saw a row of siege guns, manned and ready for action, while a dense mass of unorganized infantry were rallied to their support. No doubt they were men from every regiment on the field, rallied by brave officers for the last and final stand.

We passed them—or, at least, I did. As I reached the top of the bluff I saw, marching up, in well dressed lines, the advance of General Nelson's division of Buell's army, then being ferried across the river. They moved up the bluff and took part in repulsing the last, rather feeble assault made at dark by a small portion of the enemy, though the main defence was made by brave men collected from every quarter of the field, determined to fight to the last.

As for myself, I was alone in the crowd. My regiment was thoroughly scattered. I was considerably hurt and demoralized, and didn't take a hand in the last repulse of the enemy. Darkness came on, and then, for the first time since morning, the horrid din of fire-arms ceased. An examination showed that the ball, though it had hit me fair on the rib, was so far spent that it only made a bad bruise and respiration painful. A requisition on the sugar and hard tack followed, and then, as I happened to be near an old house filled with wounded, most of the night was spent in carrying them water.

Every fifteen minutes the horizon was lighted up by the flash of a great gun from one of our gunboats, as it sent a shell over towards the Confederate bivouacs in the woods. General Lew Wallace's division at last reached the battle field, and was placed by General Grant on the right, preparatory to renewing the fight in the morning. All night long the fresh divisions of Buell's army were being ferried across the river, and placed in position. A light rain came on, putting out the fires kindled by the battle.

The next morning the contest was begun by Wallace's division of Buell's army. The remnants of Grant's army that had any fight left in them, slowly collected together on the right.

My own regiment, when I found its colours, had as many men together, probably, as any in Hurlbut's division, but there could not have been more than one hundred and fifty. It was the same, I suspect, with every regiment that had been hotly engaged. The men were thoroughly scattered. Soldiers of pluck joined us who could not find their own command, and no doubt some of ours joined other regiments.

When our general was again about to lead our division to the front, I was only too glad to avail myself of permission to join a body of men to support a battery in reserve. Badly bruised, sore and worn out, I sat or lay on the ground near the guns, while Monday's battle progressed, the sound of it getting farther and farther away. About two o'clock we saw the cavalry moving to the front, and knew the enemy had retreated.

That night, as we collected on our old camp ground, what eager inquiries were made! With what welcome did we greet each new arrival; how excitedly the events of the last two days were discussed! We found that from the fourteen in our tent, one was killed, one mortally wounded, and seven others more or less severely wounded, only five escaping unhurt. This proportion, of course, was very unusual. The regiment itself, which had not lost many in the first two fights we made, was still, on account of the disastrous retreat under a flank fire, one of the heaviest losers, in proportion to the numbers engaged, in the whole army.

The feeling in the army after the battle was very bitter. All felt that even a few hours' notice of the impending attack, spent in preparation to receive it, would have been ample to have enabled us to give the Confederates such a reception as Beauregard feared and expected, and to have defeated them. It was long before General Grant regained the confidence of the army and country that he lost that day. He and

Sherman here learned a lesson that they never forgot, but they learned it at fearful cost to the country and to us.

It has been many times claimed that Buell's opportune arrival Sunday night saved Grant and his army from annihilation on Monday. This is probably correct. Still, it is possible, that without this aid, the arrival on the ground of Lew Wallace's fresh and strong division, to aid the thousands of brave men determined to fight to the last, would have resulted in the repulse of an enemy which had suffered so severely on Sunday.

But I have long been inclined to agree with these Southerners, who contend, that if the gallant Johnston had not been killed so early in the afternoon, our defeat would have been accomplished long enough before dark, to have rendered our reinforcements useless.

One word more, as to the numbers of the armies engaged on Sunday. A careful comparison of the returns will show that at the beginning the two armies were about equally matched in numbers; but by the time our stampeded men had got out of the way, and the two reserve divisions were in line with the remnants of the three other divisions, the preponderance was largely with the Confederates. They could choose their own point of attack, and we had no reserve with which to strengthen a shattered line.

The literature of the battle is quite extensive. The Count of Paris gives in his history the best preliminary description; but as a whole, and making reasonable allowances, the best account yet written is contained in the life of Albert Sidney Johnston, by his son. The account by General Force, contained in the Scribner series of "Campaigns of the Civil War," is good.

But no study of the battle can be complete without the aid of General Buell's articles in the Century Magazine, and the maps of the field, which he has so carefully prepared.

What were the results of this first great battle of the war? Its influence upon the gigantic contest which was to be waged for three years longer was probably not great. It was too near a drawn battle. But if it was necessary to demonstrate to the world and to ourselves the courage of our people, that generations of peace and peaceful pursuits had not one whit lessened the force or the enthusiasm of the race that peopled this Western Continent, then here was demonstration the most positive.

The people of the South for the first time realized the nature of the conflict they had provoked. Until this campaign, the great mass of the Southerners could not be made to believe that the students and farmers and mechanics and merchants of the North loved their country and its institutions more than they loved the gains of peace; nay, more than they loved their lives. They saw here an army of young men representing their kindred of the North, fighting, not for their own homes and firesides, but for the perpetuity of the Nation, with a courage and pertinacity which showed that this generation was resolved to transmit what it had received from the fathers of the country. They saw this army attacked at every disadvantage, rally at the call of a chief worthy of it, and who was a type of its character and its lofty motives, and then bravely endure a storm unparalleled on this continent.

The thousands of youthful dead left on that bloody battlefield demonstrated that we have a country and a race worthy to take the lead in the march of human advancement.

Warren Olney.

Battle of Shiloh

Joseph W. Rich

Contents

Original Editor's Introduction

In the Battle of Shiloh there is much to interest the student of Iowa history. This State had more men in the conflict, in proportion to its population, than any other. Eleven Iowa regiments of infantry were engaged, namely: the Second, the Third, the Sixth, the Seventh, the Eighth, the Eleventh, the Twelfth, the Thirteenth, the Fourteenth, the Fifteenth, and the Sixteenth. Besides these regiments there were in the Twenty-fifth Missouri, which was the regiment that furnished the reconnoitring party sent out on Sunday morning, April 6th, three Iowa companies, namely: Company F, Company I, and Company K.

The Sixth Iowa Regiment claims the distinction of being the first regiment to disembark at Pittsburg Landing, and the Eighth claims the distinction of being the last regiment to retire from the line in the Hornets' Nest. Five Iowa regiments were in the Hornets' Nest; and three of the number, the Eighth, the Twelfth, and the Fourteenth, were captured. All of the other Iowa regiments were in the thick of the conflict on Sunday.

Before the close of the war there were promotions of both officers and men from among those engaged in the Battle of Shiloh; while several participants attained civil distinction during and after the war. Major Wm. M. Stone of the Third Regiment and Lieutenant Buren R. Sherman of the Thirteenth Regiment served the State as Governor. Sherman served as Auditor of State three terms before becoming Governor. Major W. W. Belknap of the Fifteenth Regiment became Secretary of War; and Lieutenant David B. Henderson of the Twelfth Regiment, after long service in the lower house of Congress, became Speaker. Many others from Iowa who engaged in the battle served the State in the General Assembly, in Congress, and in other official stations of responsibility.

Mr. Joseph W. Rich, the author of this monograph, was himself a participant in the battle as a member of Company E of the Twelfth Iowa Regiment. He had enlisted on October 1, 1861, for the term of three years; but about the middle of his term of service he was discharged from the hospital on surgeon's certificate of disability. Having been on the field during both days of the battle and having subsequently (in 1908) gone over the ground with Major D. W. Reed, Secretary of the Shiloh National Military Park Commission, Mr. Rich has been able to bring to these pages the first-hand information of an eye witness as well as the evidences of documentary sources.

This account of the Battle of Shiloh first appeared in the October, 1909, number of *The Iowa Journal of History and Politics,* and has received most favourable comment from such men as General Frederick D. Grant, General Grenville M. Dodge, General Charles Morton, and General John H. Stibbs. Indeed, it is not often that a writer of history succeeds in being so accurate in his presentation of facts and so fair and non-partisan in his judgments as to satisfy those who, as participants in or as special students of the events described, have or believe they have first-hand information. Mr. Rich is, therefore, to be congratulated upon the uniformly favourable criticism which followed the first appearance of his monograph.

Benj. F. Shambaugh

Office of the Superintendent and Editor
The State Historical Society of Iowa
Iowa City 1911

Author's Preface

No apology is offered for the appearance of another paper on the Battle of Shiloh, for the reason that the last word to be said on the subject has not been said, and indeed will not have been said until the last serious misrepresentation, made through ignorance, prejudice, malice, or for any other reason, has been corrected. It is not in the thought of the writer that he will be able to contribute additional facts to the literature of the subject; but it is hoped that the facts may be so grouped and illustrated as to leave a clearer picture of the battle in the mind of the reader.

As far as the writer knows the movements of the battle on Sunday, April 6, 1862, have not heretofore been illustrated except by means of one general map, showing progressive movements of the battle lines throughout the day. Such a map can be little better than a puzzle-picture to the general reader.

The original map from which the tracings were made to illustrate the Battle of Shiloh was prepared under direction of the Shiloh National Military Park Commission, to accompany its account of the battle, entitled *The Battle of Shiloh and the Organizations Engaged*, compiled from official records by Major D. W. Reed, Historian and Secretary of the Commission. To insure accuracy in the original map, the field was carefully platted by the Commission's engineer, Mr. Atwell Thompson, and the camps and battle lines were located by Major D. W. Reed, after an exhaustive study of official documents, aided by the recollections of scores of officers and men engaged in the battle on the respective sides.

The reader must remember, however, that the lines were never for a moment stationary, so that it would be a physical impossibility to represent them correctly at short intervals of time. The analysis here given of the general map published by the Commission, it is believed, will aid materially in understanding the battle.

Though not offering an apology for this paper, the writer is disposed to justify its appearance somewhat by referring briefly, by way of introduction, to a few illustrative errors and misrepresentations sought to be corrected, pointing out some of the so-called histories and memoirs where they are to be found. Of course it is not to be presumed that these errors and misrepresentations were intentional: they are due mainly to two causes—to the "smart" newspaper correspondent, whose main object was sensation; and to the unreliable historian whose main weakness was indolence in searching for facts. Prejudice may in a few cases have contributed to the pollution of the historic stream.

Special acknowledgments are due from the writer to Major D. W. Reed, Secretary and Historian of the Shiloh National Military Park Commission, for valuable suggestions in the preparation of this paper. The writer is also under obligations to Lieutenant Wm. J. Hahn of Omaha, Nebraska, a member of the Twenty-fifth Missouri, who was of the Major Powell reconnoitring party, sent out by Colonel Peabody on Sunday morning, April 6th; and also to T. W. Holman of Rutledge, Missouri, who was a member of the Twenty-first Missouri Infantry and was with the regiment when it went out to re-enforce the reconnoitring party and the pickets.

Joseph W. Rich

The State Historical Society of Iowa
Iowa City

The Battle of Shiloh

One of the worst as it was one of the first of the sensational stories of the Battle of Shiloh put in historic form was the account by Horace Greeley in his *American Conflict*. The camp at Pittsburg Landing before the battle is likened to a Methodist camp-meeting, and the Union army on Sunday morning is represented as a "bewildered, half-dressed, ... helpless, coatless, musketless mob", upon which the enemy sprang "with the bayonet". This account has Prentiss's division "routed before it had time to form a line of battle;" and Sherman's division is "out of the fight by 8 o'clock". [1]

J. S. C. Abbott in his story of the Battle of Shiloh as given in his two-volume *History of the Civil War*, gathered his material from the same sensational sources and he used it in the same sensational way as did Mr. Greeley.

A more pretentious work, which appeared much later, was Scribners' *History of the United States* in five volumes. This work appeared after original sources of information had become easily accessible; and yet in its account of the Battle of Shiloh it is the sinner of sinners for untruthfulness. It is no exaggeration to say of the Scribners' account of the battle what General Beauregard is credited with having said of General Halleck's report to the Secretary of War at Washington as to the condition of the Confederate army after the evacuation of Corinth—"it contains more lies than lines".

Another of the sensational type, though of pretentious title, is Headley's *History of the Rebellion*. Headley represents the Union officers as still in bed, when the "inundation" came, and says that "the troops seizing their muskets as they could, fled like a herd of sheep". Unfortunately for the reputation of Mr. Headley as a historian, the facts are all against him—he allowed himself to be misled by the fic-

---

1 Greeley's *The American Conflict*, Vol. 2, pp. 58-61.

tion-writers.

John Codman Ropes, who enjoys something of a reputation as a critical writer, in his recent *Story of the Civil War*, published by the Massachusetts Historical Society, shows plainly that he followed very closely the account as given by General Buell, in his *Shiloh Reviewed*; and he shows, also, a prejudiced judgment against Grant and in favour of Buell—whom he evidently admired. Mr. Ropes makes it appear that none of the divisions near the Landing were in line until after Sherman and Prentiss had fallen back from their first lines, about ten a. m. He leaves it to be inferred also that Buell had an entire division on the west side of the river and in the fight on Sunday night; and he figures that not more than five thousand of Grant's five divisions, which were engaged in the battle on Sunday, were in line at the close of the day.

John Fiske is another writer on Civil War subjects, and in his *Mississippi Valley in the Civil War* he describes the Battle of Shiloh, but not without some rather serious errors. For instance he attributes the "wait-for-Buell" policy to Grant—it was due to his superior, General Halleck. He says that General McClernand was the ranking officer at Pittsburg Landing in General Grant's absence, which is not correct—General Sherman was the ranking officer. He makes no mention of the reconnoitring party that went out from Prentiss's division before daylight on Sunday morning, but says that "when the Confederates attacked in full force on Sunday morning, the Federals were in camp and not in line of battle."On the same page, however, he gives himself a flat contradiction by telling how Prentiss had formed line and advanced a quarter of a mile, where he received "the mighty rush of the Confederates"—and the time he fixes at about half past five o'clock, which is an error of fully two hours.

On one page he gives the strength of the Confederate army as 36,000, exclusive of cavalry, and on another page his "reckoning" is 30,000 on the same basis. He criticises General Johnston for giving so much attention to the divisions of Prentiss and Sherman, at the opening of the battle, when he should have massed heavily against Stuart, the extreme left of the Union line, forgetting, if he ever knew, that Prentiss and Sherman must be forced back before Stuart could be attacked. The plan suggested by Fiske would have exposed the Confederate flank to the two divisions of Prentiss and Sherman, which would have been a blunder. The corps organization of the Confederate army appears, by inference, to have been well maintained; whereas they began to commingle at the beginning of the battle, and the corps were practically broken up by ten o'clock.

Mr. Fiske is again in error in leaving the inference that an entire brigade of Nelson's division was in at the close of the fight on Sunday night. And still another error is the statement that three Confederate brigades participated in the last attack near the Landing. He gives the number of guns in Grant's last line far below the facts, and then speculates upon what might have been if General Beauregard could have "put 6,000 to 8,000 fresh reserves into the fight against his weary antagonist", apparently never thinking of the converse of the speculation. Mr. Fiske appears to be particularly unfortunate in the handling of statistics. He makes it appear that Lew. Wallace brought 7,000 men to Grant's right, and Nelson about the same number to his left, on Sunday night—an error of 4,000 or more. If Mr. Fiske had trusted less to *Shiloh Reviewed* and more to official records, he would have made fewer mistakes.

Henry Villard, who was a newspaper correspondent with Buell's army, has written what he calls *Memoirs*, and "in order to impart greater accuracy and perhaps some novelty," to his "sketch" of the Battle of Shiloh, he goes to Confederate reports for his information. His "sketch" abounds in errors, even to the misquoting of one of General Grant's dispatches, thus changing a negative to an affirmative statement.

As recently as 1895 a Brevet Brigadier General, U. S.V., Henry M. Cist, in his *Army of the Cumberland*, quotes approvingly from Comte de Paris's *History of the Civil War* as follows:

> At the sight of the enemy's batteries advancing in good order, the soldiers that have been grouped together in haste, to give an air of support to Webster's batteries, became frightened, and scattered. It is about to be carried, when a new body of troops deploying in the rear of the guns .... received the Confederates with a fire that drives them back in disorder. [2]

Mr. Cist quotes also from Whitelaw Reid's *Ohio in the War* as follows:

> He [Buell] came into the action when, without him, all was lost. He redeemed the fortunes of the field, and justly won the title of the 'Hero of Pittsburg Landing' [3]

---

2 Cist's *The Army of the Cumberland*, pp. 74, 75.
3 Cist's *The Army of the Cumberland*, p. 77.

Of the second quotation it needs only to be said that its author was the newspaper correspondent who wrote the first sensational and untruthful account of the Battle of Shiloh. The other quotation may well pass for an Arabian Nights tale.

General Lew. Wallace, commanding the second division of Grant's army, having his camp at Crump's Landing six miles down the river from Pittsburg Landing, has left for us his *Autobiography*, which in many respects is an interesting work. But if it is to be judged by its account of the Battle of Shiloh, in which Wallace participated on the second day, the author's reputation as a writer of fiction will not suffer. General Wallace accepts the first stories as to the "complete surprise" of the camp and offers argument to prove the contention. Then he proceeds to upset his own argument by showing that Prentiss and Sherman had their divisions in line of battle before six o'clock, or before the Confederate lines began to move to the attack. He brings the advance of Buell's army on the field some three hours before it was actually there; has General W. H. L. Wallace mortally wounded about the same length of time before the incident occurred; has General Johnston killed in front of the Hornets' Nest.

He credits the men in the Hornets' Nest with holding the position "for two or three hours," whereas it was "held" from about 9:30 a. m. to about 5:30 p. m. "against the choicest chivalry of the South, led by General Johnston himself," to quote General Wallace. In fact, General Johnston led no assault upon the Hornets' Nest, or upon any other position in the Union line. These are a few of many fictions in Wallace's *Autobiography*, where, of all places, the truth should be found.

Had it been true that the position at the Hornets ' Nest was held "for two or three hours" only, Grant's centre would have been broken while Nelson's division was still ten miles away, and about the hour when Wallace's division started on its fifteen mile march. In that event, the story of the Battle of Shiloh would have been a different story. Grant's army would, probably, have been defeated, and Buell's army then strung out over thirty miles of country road, might easily have suffered the same fate. Fortunately, General Wallace was writing fiction.

At the risk of tediousness one more writer on the Battle of Shiloh will be mentioned. General Buell, who participated in the battle of the second day, in a carefully prepared paper, entitled *Shiloh Reviewed*[4], takes the position of an advocate before a court and jury, stating what

---

4 *The Century Magazine*, Vol. 31, p. 749.

he expects to prove, then marshalling his facts—or fictions, as the case may be—to make good his contention. He opens his case with the following proposition: "At the moment near the close of the day when the remnant of the retrograding army was driven to refuge in the midst of its magazines, with the triumphant enemy at half -gunshot distance, the advance division of a re-enforcing army arrived . . . . and took position under fire at the point of attack; the attacking force was checked, and the battle ceased for the day." The reader, not familiar with the facts, must necessarily draw two inferences from this statement: (1) that an entire division of Buell's army was "at the point of attack"; (2) that the presence of such a body of fresh troops decided the fate of the day. Both inferences are erroneous, as the facts will show.

On one point of some importance, General Buell flatly contradicts himself. In speaking of the attack near the Landing, Sunday night, he says, in *Shiloh Reviewed*, that the "fire of the gunboats was harmless". In his official report written just after the battle, he says that the "gunboats contributed very much to the result"—the repulse of the enemy.

Perhaps a perfectly fair and unprejudiced account of the Battle of Shiloh ought not to have been expected from the pen of General Buell. He had, or fancied that he had, grievances against both General Grant and General Halleck—and he was human.

THE BATTLE OF SHILOH NOT AN ISOLATED INCIDENT

The Battle of Shiloh was not an isolated incident: it was one of a series of incidents, more or less closely related, in which the Army of the Tennessee figured prominently and effectively, but with divided responsibilities. It is, therefore, proper to take into account conditions precedent to the battle before passing judgment upon the men and the commanders who happened to be present at the moment, and upon whom fell the immediate responsibilities, and who suffered for the shortcomings of others.

The Army of the Tennessee was at Pittsburg Landing under the orders of an officer superior in rank to the officer in immediate command; and it was there for a definite purpose. If it did not accomplish the definite purpose, it may be answered, in extenuation at least, that it was not permitted to try—its hands were tied and it was ordered to "wait". It waited until compelled to fight for its own safety. It saved itself from defeat and, very probably, saved from destruction another army of equal strength.

It is of no consequence who first suggested the line of the Tennessee and Cumberland rivers as the weak point in the Confederate line between Columbus on the West and Bowling Green on the East. It would have been a reflection on military genius, if the suggestion had not come to several persons at about the same time—so patent was the evidence. It is of some importance, however, to remember who made the first move to save the "weak point". Just seven months before the Battle of Shiloh (September 6, 1861), the first direct step was taken leading to that event.

On September 4, 1861, General Grant took command of the Cairo district with headquarters at Cairo, General Fremont being then department commander with headquarters at St. Louis. On the day after taking command of the district, General Grant learned of an expedition from Columbus to occupy Paducah at the mouth of the Tennessee. A force was at once prepared to anticipate the Confederate movement; a dispatch was then sent to headquarters that the force would move at a certain hour unless orders were received to the contrary. No order came back, and Paducah was occupied without firing a shot on the next morning much to the surprise of the inhabitants who were hourly expecting the Confederates then on the march. General Grant returned to Cairo on the same day, finding there the order permitting him to do what was already done. The same movement that saved the Tennessee saved also the Cumberland.

Except for this prompt action on the part of General Grant the mouths of these two rivers would surely have been strongly fortified; but, instead, the Confederate line was forced back a hundred miles, in its centre, to Fort Henry on the Tennessee and Fort Donelson on the Cumberland (Map 1).

Columbus, a few miles below Cairo, strongly fortified and garrisoned by the Confederates, was so situated that it might, unless threatened from Cairo and Paducah, throw troops either west into Missouri or east by rail to Bowling Green or to points within easy marching distance of Fort Henry and Fort Donelson as there might be need. As a result of these conditions, there was activity in Grant's district, during the fall and winter months of 1861. The battle of Belmont (Nov. 7, 1861) was one of the "diversions" to keep the garrison at Columbus at home. In the following January, General Halleck having become department commander, expeditions were sent out from Cairo and Paducah to the rear of Columbus and up the west bank of the

Tennessee—General C. F. Smith commanding the latter expedition. General Smith, having scouted as far toward Fort Henry as he thought advisable, went on board the gunboat *Lexington* "to have a look" at the Fort. The gunboat went within "about 2½ miles drawing a single shot from the enemy in response to four several shots fired at them." In his report (Jan. 22, 1862) to General Grant, General Smith said: "I think two iron-clad gunboats would make short work of Fort Henry." [5]

On the same day that General Smith reported on Fort Henry, General Grant was given "permission to visit headquarters" in response to a request made some time before—but he soon learned that advice and suggestions in regard to affairs in his district were not wanted, and he went back to his command. He ventured, however (Jan. 28th) to send the following to his superior:

> With permission, I will take Fort Henry . . . and establish and hold a large camp there.[6]

Permission was granted on the 30th, and Grant was "off up the Tennessee" (February 2nd).

Except for this appeal for "permission" to take Fort Henry, backed by the advice of Flag-Officer Foote, commanding the gunboat flotilla, the expedition would have been delayed at least two weeks, giving that much more time for the Confederates to strengthen themselves. On the day after the surrender of Fort Henry (February 6) Halleck telegraphed to Buell that he "had no idea of commencing the movement before the 15th or the 20th instant".[7] And he was evidently very uneasy about the success of the movement, as appears from a dispatch sent to the General-in-Chief (McClellan) at Washington at the very moment when Foote's guns were pounding at the little mud fort. The dispatch was as follows:

> If you can give me . . . . 10,000 more men, I will take Fort Henry, cut the enemy's line, and paralyze Columbus. Give me 25,000 and I will threaten Nashville .... so as to force the enemy to abandon Bowling Green without a battle.[8]

Before that dispatch was received in Washington the thing was accomplished by a gunboat bombardment of an hour and fifteen minutes at Fort Henry.

---

5 *War of the Rebellion*: Official Records, Series 1, Vol. 7 p. 561.
6 *War of the Rebellion*: Official Records, Series 1, Vol. 7 p. 121.
7 *War of the Rebellion*: Official Records, Series 1, Vol. 7 p. 593.
8 *War of the Rebellion*: Official Records, Series 1, Vol. 7 p. 587.

Notwithstanding the fact that the expedition against Fort Henry was undertaken before Halleck was ready for it and the fact that he had misgivings as to its success, he yet seems to have been jealous lest Buell might share in the honours in case of success. When Buell learned of the movement, which was undertaken without consultation with him, he telegraphed Halleck to know if "co-operation" on his part was "essential to .... success," to which Halleck replied: "Co-operation at present not essential." [9] Buell was piqued at Halleck's reply, and telegraphed to the General-in-Chief: "I protest against such prompt proceedings, as though I had nothing to do but command 'Commence firing' when he starts off." [10]

This episode is mentioned only for the purpose of showing that there were personal complications between these three commanders that, possibly, had some bearing on the Battle of Shiloh. The affairs of the succeeding three weeks, after Fort Henry, did but complicate the complications, and upon General Grant fell the unfavourable results.

No person was more surprised than was General Halleck at the success of the expedition to Fort Henry, but he continued to appeal to the General-in-Chief for "more troops" while Grant was preparing to advance upon Fort Donelson and after the investment of that place: (February 8th) without more troops, "I cannot advance on Nashville"; (February 10th) "Do send me more troops. It is the crisis of the war in the West"; (February 14th) "Can't you spare some troops from the Potomac?"[11]

Two days after the last appeal, Fort Donelson surrendered, and Clarksville and Nashville waited only to be "occupied". They were occupied, respectively, on the 21st and 25th, without opposition. Nashville was occupied by Nelson's division of Buell's army which was sent to re-enforce Grant at Donelson; but, arriving too late, it was sent directly forward to Nashville by order of Grant, the latter following in person for the purpose of conferring with Buell—and this last move came near being the undoing of General Grant who mortally offended his superior by pushing the campaign too rapidly, arousing at the same time the jealousy of Buell by occupying Nashville just ahead of his [Buell's] army approaching from the North. General Grant was in "ahead of the hounds," at Nashville—that was his only offense.

---

9 *War of the Rebellion*: Official Records, Series 1, Vol. 7 pp. 574, 576.
10 *War of the Rebellion*: Official Records, Series 1, Vol. 7 p. 933.
11 *War of the Rebellion*: Official Records, Series 1, Vol. 7 pp. 594, 599, 612.

On the day that Nashville was occupied by the Union troops (February 25) the Confederates began the evacuation of Columbus, the last defence on the original line, and began at once to establish a new line along the Mobile and Ohio Railroad from Columbus southward to Corinth and from Memphis eastward through Corinth to Chattanooga on the Memphis and Charleston Railroad, with General Beauregard in command, Corinth being the strategical point at the crossing of the two roads (Map 1).

After the evacuation of Nashville the Confederates under General Johnston moved southward as rapidly as possible, striking the Memphis and Charleston road at Decatur, thence moving west to Corinth, the advance reaching that place March 18th. General Johnston reached Corinth on the 24th, assuming command of the combined Confederate forces on the 29th.

The commanders of the two Union armies, Halleck and Buell, after Nashville, did not fully agree as to the best plan of following up the advantages already gained. Buell thought, with the General-in-Chief (McClellan), that Chattanooga was of "next importance" after Nashville[12] and he prepared to follow Johnston south. Halleck thought that the line of the Tennessee River offered the opportunity to strike the enemy's centre at or near Corinth[13] and he urged Buell to join him in that movement, but without avail. A few days later, however, General Halleck secured what he had long-desired, the consolidation of the two Departments with himself in command. Halleck urged his claims on two grounds: (1) that all of the armies of the West should be under one command, and (2) that the command should fall to him in recognition of the successful campaign against Fort Henry and Fort Donelson in his Department.[14] The consolidation took place on March 11th, after which date General Buell was subject to orders from St. Louis, as General Grant had been from the first. General Buell's advance southward from Nashville had reached Columbia on Duck River before the consolidation (March 10), but his headquarters were still at Nashville.

On the first of March it appears that General Halleck notified General Grant that his column would move "up the Tennessee", and

---

12 *War of the Rebellion:* Official Records, Series I, Vol. 7 p. 660.
13 *War of the Rebellion:* Official Records, Series I, Vol. 10, Part 2, p. 38.
14 *War of the Rebellion:* Official Records, Series I, Vol. 7, p. 628.

that the main object would be "to destroy the railroad bridge over Bear Creek, near Eastport . . . . and also the connections at Corinth, Jackson, and Humboldt." He was instructed to "Avoid any general engagement with strong forces better retreat than to risk a general battle." [15] Two days later, General Halleck sent to the General-in-Chief the complaint against General Grant, which resulted in the latter's practical suspension from active command, Halleck suggesting at the same time that General C. F. Smith command the expedition up the Tennessee. In response to Halleck's complaint, he was authorized to put General Grant under arrest, "if the good of the service requires it", to which Halleck replied: "I do not deem it advisable to arrest him at present". [16]

On the fourth of March, Halleck dispatched to Grant:

You will place Maj. Gen. C. F. Smith in command of expedition and remain yourself at Fort Henry.

To this, Grant replied, on the next day:

Troops will be sent, under command of Major-General Smith, as directed. I had prepared a different plan, intending General Smith to command the forces which will go to Paris and Humboldt, while I would command the expedition upon Eastport, Corinth, and Jackson in person.

He then assures General Halleck that instructions will be carried out "to the very best" of his ability. [17]

Under this order of his superior, General Grant remained at Fort Henry, acting in the capacity of a forwarding-officer, until the 17th of the month—the most important two weeks between the date of the order to proceed up the Tennessee and the 6th of April following, when the camp was attacked at Pittsburg Landing. The expedition was planned without consultation with General Grant, commander of the district, and it was directed, except in minor details, from headquarters in St. Louis both before and after March 17th—the date of General Grant's restoration to active command of the army in the field.

The expedition left Fort Henry on March 9th under command of General Smith, with full authority from the Department commander to select the place of landing. [18] General Smith established headquar-

15 *War of the Rebellion*: Official Records, Series 1, Vol. 7, p. 674.
16 *War of the Rebellion*: Official Records, Series 1 Vol. 7, pp. 680, 682.
17 *War of the Rebellion*: Official Records, Series 1, Vol. 10. Part 2, pp. 3-5
18 *War of the Rebellion*: Official Records, Series 1, Vol. 10, Part 2, pp. 21-26.

ters at Savannah, on the east bank of the river, but sent one division (General Lew. Wallace) five miles farther up to Crump's Landing on the west bank of the river, where his division went into camp on the 12th. On the 13th Wallace sent an expedition west about fifteen miles to the Mobile and Ohio Railway near Bethel station, where about a half-mile of trestle work was destroyed.[19] The damage to the road was slight, however, as repairs were soon made (Map 1).

On the 14th General Smith reported that he had "not been able to get anything like the desired information as to the strength of the enemy, but it seems to be quoted at 50,000 to 60,000 from Jackson through Corinth and farther east." It was this information that induced General Smith "not to attempt to cut the communication at that place, [Corinth] as that would inevitably lead to a collision in numbers" that he was "ordered to avoid". [20]

Immediately after this report was made, General Sherman was ordered with his division to a point some distance above Pittsburg Landing, with instructions to cut the Memphis and Charleston road, if possible, at some point east of Corinth. The attempt failed on account of high water and Sherman dropped back to Pittsburg Landing, where he met Hurlbut's division sent up by General Smith as support in case of need. The two divisions left the boats at Pittsburg Landing and went into camp. General Sherman sent out a strong reconnoitring force toward Corinth, and on the 17th he reported to General Smith: "I am satisfied we cannot reach the Memphis and Charleston Road without a considerable engagement, which is prohibited by General Halleck's instructions, so that I will be governed by your orders of yesterday to occupy Pittsburg strongly." [21]

General Lew. Wallace, whose division was at Crump's Landing at this time, says in his *Autobiography* that if General Smith had received the order from Halleck that he expected, to move directly on Corinth, "there had been no battle of Shiloh." And again he says that by the time General Grant was restored to command, the opportunity of ad

General Grant was restored to active command on March 17th, and going at once to General Smith's headquarters at Savannah he reported on the 18th the distribution of troops as he found it—three

---

19 *War of the Rebellion: Official Records*, Series 1, Vol. 10, Part 1, pp. 9, 10.
20 *War of the Rebellion: Official Records*, Series 1, Vol. 10. Part 1, p. 8.
21 *War of the Rebellion: Official Records*, Series 1, Vol. 10. Part 1, p. 25.22 Wallace's *Autobiography*, Vol. 1, pp. 446, 451.

divisions on the west side of the Tennessee, Sherman and Hurlbut at Pittsburg Landing, and Lew. Wallace at Crump's Landing; at Savannah, on the east side of the river was McClernand's division; and on transports on the river, waiting for orders, were several regiments which were ordered to Pittsburg Landing.

It is important to remember this distribution of the army as General Grant found it, under the sanction if not the direct order of the Department commander. That General Halleck still believed it possible to cut the Memphis and Charleston Railroad, according to his original plan, is shown by a dispatch to General Grant (March 18th) based on a rumour to the effect that the enemy had moved from Corinth to attack the line of the Tennessee below Savannah, that is, to attack Grant's communications.

"If so," says General Halleck, "General Smith should immediately destroy railroad connections at Corinth." [23] To this General Grant replied on the 19th: "Immediate preparations will be made to execute your . . . . order. I will go in person". [24]

Again, on the next day in a lengthy dispatch to Halleck's Adjutant General, Grant repeated his intention to go "in person" with the expedition "should no orders received hereafter prevent it"—adding that he would "take no risk . . . . under the instructions" which he already had; that if a battle seemed to be inevitable, he could "make a movement upon some other point of the railroad .... and thus save the demoralizing effect of a retreat". [25]

General Halleck evidently thought there was special significance in Grant's intention to "go in person" with the expedition toward Corinth—he knew something would be doing—so, on the 20th Halleck dispatched: "keep your forces together until you connect with General Buell . . . . Don't let the enemy draw you into an engagement now." [26]

Before this last dispatch was received, orders were issued by General Grant to all division commanders to hold themselves ready to march at a moment's notice, with three days' rations in haversacks and seven days' rations in wagons. On receiving the "wait" order, Grant dispatched again (March 21): "Corinth cannot be taken without meeting a large force, say 30,000. A general engagement would be inevitable;

23 *War of the Rebellion*: Official Records, Series 1, Vol. 10, Part 2, p. 46.

24 *War of the Rebellion*: Official Records, Series 1, Vol. 10, Part 2, p. 49.

25 *War of the Rebellion*: Official Records, Series 1, Vol. 10, Part 2, p. 51.

26 *War of the Rebellion*: Official Records, Series 1, Vol. 10, Part 2, pp. 50-51.

therefore I will wait a few days for further instructions."[27] Evidently General Grant was restive and anxious, believing that precious time was going to waste, as appears from what he wrote to General Smith: "the sooner we attack the easier will be the task". [28]

As far as the records show, no orders later than March 20th were received by General Grant; and so the army within striking distance of the enemy was in a state of suspended animation for nearly three weeks. The army was expected to cut the Memphis and Charleston road, but it was not permitted to fight for the purpose; it must do it without disturbing the enemy.

It is important to remember in this connection that the territory west of the Tennessee River, from near its mouth southward to Pittsburg Landing and west to the Mississippi, was the enemy's country both in sentiment and by strong military occupation, and so the expedition under General Smith up the Tennessee was moving fully two hundred miles from its base of supplies, wholly dependent upon the river. This territory was well supplied with railroads under control of the enemy, by means of which, if so disposed, he might throw a strong force on short notice against General Smith's communications. General Grant evidently had this danger in mind when replying to General Halleck's order sending the expedition up the river, as already quoted. But in this as in other things, General Grant's advice was not sought and his suggestions were not heeded. The conditions at Pittsburg Landing were not of his making—they were accepted as they were found, even after three requests to be relieved of command in the Department, because of the strained relations between his superior and himself. [29]

General Buell's Movements

In pursuance of his plan after Nashville, to follow the enemy south, on March 10th, General Buell reported his advance at Columbia, Tennessee, at the crossing of Duck River. [30] The consolidation of the two Departments occurred on the 11th, and on the 13th, General Halleck, as if in some degree appreciating General Buell's embarrassment, wrote him as follows:

---

27 *War of the Rebellion*: Official Records, Series 1, Vol. 10, Part 2, p. 55.

28 *War of the Rebellion*: Official Records, Series 1, Vol. 10. Part 2, p. 62.

29 The several requests to be relieved of command in Halleck's department bear date of March 7, 9, and 11.—*War of the Rebellion*: Official Records, Series 1, Vol. 10, Part 2, pp. 15, 21, 30.

30 *War of the Rebellion*: Official Records, Series 1, Vol. 10, Part 2, p. 25.

The new arrangement of departments will not interfere with your command. You will continue in command of the same army and district of country as heretofore, so far as I am concerned. [31]

Definite orders to General Buell soon followed the consolidation; March 16th:

Move your forces by land to the Tennessee .... Grant's army is concentrating at Savannah.

Again on March 20th:

Important that you communicate with General Smith as soon as possible.

And again on March 29th:

You will concentrate all your available troops at Savannah, or Pittsburg, 12 miles above.[32]

As already stated, General Buell had one division at Columbia—about forty miles on the road to Savannah—when the order came to join Grant. The remainder of the army moved promptly, but was detained at the crossing of Duck River in building a bridge until the 30th, though one division (Nelson's) waded the river on the 29th.

Naturally General Grant, in front of a rapidly concentrating army under General Johnston and General Beauregard, was anxious to know of General Buell's movements, and so, two days after assuming active command, two couriers were started from Savannah for Buell's camp which was reached on the 23rd with this dispatch from Grant:

I am massing troops at Pittsburg, Tennessee. There is every reason to suppose that the rebels have a large force at Corinth, Miss., and many at other points on the road toward Decatur.[33]

Thus General Buell had positive knowledge both from General Halleck and General Grant that the latter was "massing troops" at Pittsburg Landing—and this information was in possession of General Buell a full week before his army was able to cross Duck River (about 90 miles away) and two weeks before the battle. This point is dwelt upon for the reason that certain writers have erroneously claimed that General Buell had not been informed of General Grant's position on

---

31 *War of the Rebellion*: Official Records, Series 1, Vol. 10. Part 2, p. 33.
32 *War of the Rebellion*: Official Records, Series 1, Vol. 10, Part 2, pp. 42, 51, 77.
33 *War of the Rebellion*: Official Records, Series 1, Vol. 10, Part 2, p. 47.

the west bank of the Tennessee and hence did not press his march.

After wading Duck River as stated, General Nelson's division went into camp for the night, and took up the march next morning (the 30th) reaching Savannah about noon, April 5th, having marched an average of twelve miles a day.[34] General Buell arrived in Savannah "about sundown," on the same day, but he did not make his presence known, nor was his presence known to General Grant, when the latter, with his staff, took boat next morning for the battle field after an "early breakfast" left unfinished.

It need not be matter of surprise that General Buell should be reluctant to join his army of about equal strength and independent in command with the army on the Tennessee. It was Buell's wish to strike the Tennessee higher up and conduct a campaign of his own. With this in mind he suggested to General Halleck that he [Buell] be permitted to halt and go into camp about thirty miles east of Savannah, at Waynesboro. To this suggestion General Halleck replied on the 5th: "You are right about concentrating at Waynesborough. Future movements must depend upon those of the enemy." [35] General Buell issued orders to "concentrate", but fortunately his advance had passed the point designated before the orders were delivered, and the march continued. Had it been otherwise the re-enforcing army would have been forty miles away, instead of its advance division being within ten miles, when the battle began.

It may be asked: Why did not General Buell make his presence in Savannah known to General Grant promptly on arrival? Perhaps a perfectly just answer cannot be given in view of the fact that the former was not required to "report" to the latter as a subordinate to a superior—the one was to join the other and wait for orders from a higher source than either. There was but one contingency under which any part of General Buell's army could come under General Grant's orders—an attack upon the latter. General Halleck's instructions to General Grant were (April 5th):

"You will act in concert, but he [Buell] will exercise his separate command, unless the enemy should attack you. In that case

---

34 The following is the itinerary of General Nelson's march from Columbia, as given by Colonel Ammen, commanding the advance brigade: March 30, 4 miles; March 31, 10 miles; April 1, 14 miles; April 2, 16 miles; April 3, 15 miles; April 4, 10½ miles; April 5, 9½ miles.—Ammen's *Diary* in *War of the Rebellion: Official Records*, Series 1, Vol. 10, Part 1, p. 330.

35 *War of the Rebellion: Official Records*, Series 1, Vol. 10, Part 2, pp. 94, 95.

you are authorized to take the general command." [36]

The contingency arose on the morning of the 6th.

BEFORE THE BATTLE

From the date of General Halleck's "wait" order to the date of the battle—that is from March 20th to April 6th—there were fifteen full days, during which time this positive order was in force:"My instructions not to advance must be obeyed." Nothing, therefore, remained but to watch the enemy and dodge him in case he offered battle in any considerable force. There was scarcely a day in that waiting time in which there was not reconnoitring, resulting in several light encounters. Colonel Buckland, commanding the fourth brigade of General Sherman's division, has given a good account of the condition of things at the front during the three or four days before the battle in a paper read before the Society of the Army of the Tennessee in 1881 and published in the Proceedings of the Society. [37]

On Thursday, April 3rd, three days before the battle and the day on which the Confederates marched from Corinth and surrounding camps, Colonel Buckland under orders of the division commander reconnoitred four or five miles toward Corinth, finding the enemy in such force as to deter him from attack, in view of the order to "fall back" rather than risk bringing on a general engagement. The brigade marched back without an encounter.

On the next day the picket line was attacked in front of Buckland's brigade, and a picket post was captured, consisting of a lieutenant and seven men. Colonel Buckland went out with a regiment to investigate and had two of his companies surrounded by Confederate cavalry, which was in turn surprised and routed by the re-enforcements sent to the relief of the two companies. Just as the enemy appeared to be forming for a counter attack on Buckland, the Fifth Ohio cavalry of Sherman's division came up, attacked and routed the enemy, capturing several prisoners.

This affair developed the presence of the enemy in considerable force—infantry, cavalry, and artillery. When Colonel Buckland reached the picket line, on his return to camp, he found General Sherman with several regiments awaiting him and wanting to know, with a show of displeasure, what he had been doing out in front. After hearing Colonel Buckland's account of the matter, he was ordered back to camp

---

36 *War of the Rebellion*: Official Records, Series 1,Vol. 10, Part 2, p. 94.
37 *Proceedings of the Society of the Army of the Tennessee,*Vol. 14–16, p. 71.

with his men, General Sherman accompanying the order with the remark that he might have brought on a general engagement, which is to be understood as a mild reprimand.

So particular was General Sherman to avoid censure that he required Colonel Buckland to make a written report of the incident which report was sent to General Grant.

Colonel Buckland further says that he was along the picket line several times on Saturday, the day before the battle, and saw the enemy at several points, and that the pickets reported activity near the lines. Other officers made similar observations. "It was the belief of all", says Colonel Buckland, "that the enemy intended to attack us, either during the night or early in the morning." [38] This feeling was so strong that regimental officers were instructed to have their commands in readiness for attack—the picket line was strengthened and a line of sentries was established from the picket line back to camp.

Similar evidence as to the activity of the enemy on Saturday the 5th is furnished by Captain I. P. Rumsey, a staff officer of General W. H. L. Wallace, who was riding outside the lines on that day. On returning to camp Captain Rumsey reported to Colonel Dickey, 4th Illinois cavalry, that he had seen a considerable body of Confederate cavalry. The two officers going to General Sherman's headquarters, reported the facts, to which General Sherman replied: "I know they are out there, but our hands are tied; we can't do a thing." Colonel Dickey then asked permission to take his regiment out to investigate, receiving for reply: "Dickey, if you were to go out there with your regiment you would bring on a battle in less than an hour, and we have positive orders not to be drawn into a battle until Buell comes." [39]

Colonel McPherson, Halleck's chief engineer, who was camping with the second division (W. H. L. Wallace) fully corroborates the above statements, by saying: "It was well known the enemy was approaching our lines". [40]

Apprehension of an early attack upon the camp prevailed among the subordinate officers of General Prentiss's division, as well as among those of General Sherman's division, and similar orders were given to companies and regiments to be prepared for a night or an early morning attack. And it seems now to be well settled that the rec-

38 *Proceedings of the Society of the Army of the Tennessee*, Vol. 14-16, p. 77.
39 Quoted by Major D. W. Reed in a paper published in the *Proceedings of the Society of the Army of the Tennessee*, Vol. 36, p. 216.
40 *War of the Rebellion*: Official Records, Series 1, Vol. 10, Part 1, p. 181

onnoitring party sent out from Prentiss's division before daylight on Sunday morning was sent out by Colonel Peabody of the 25th Missouri, commanding the first brigade of the division, and without the knowledge of General Prentiss.

In the history of the 25th Missouri, edited and compiled by Dr. W. A. Neal, Assistant Surgeon of the regiment, and published in 1889, appears a detailed account of the action of Colonel Peabody on the eve of the battle, as related by Lieutenant James M. Newhard, at the time Orderly Sergeant of Company E, 25th Missouri, one of the companies in the reconnoitring party. It is related that Colonel Peabody urged upon General Prentiss on Saturday the 5th that an attack was very probable and that preparation ought to be made accordingly.

As nothing was done except to strengthen pickets and guards Colonel Peabody, under the influence of a premonition that an attack would be made early in the morning and that he would not survive the battle, decided to take upon himself the responsibility of sending out a party to reconnoitre. So Major Powell, an officer of the Regular Army and Field Officer of the Day was ordered to take three companies of the 25th Missouri, start at about 3 o'clock in the morning, and march until he found the enemy. The companies constituting the party were B, H, and E, of the 25th Missouri. How and where the enemy was found will be related farther on.

Some persons will have doubts, probably, in regard to the story of Colonel Peabody's premonitions of attack, and death in battle, but there can be no doubt about the attack, or about the death of Colonel Peabody, within a few minutes after the main battle began. Major Powell was also killed early in the battle, and so the two principal actors in the first scene of the drama passed quickly off the stage, but not until after the chief of the two was severely reprimanded, at the head of his brigade in line and waiting for orders. The following letter, to a nephew of Colonel Peabody, here given by permission, tells the story.

333 Highland Av.
Somerville, Mass. Feb'y. 27th 1902

Mr. F. E. Peabody,
Box 7 Boston.
Dear Sir:
Referring to our conversation concerning the Battle of Pittsburg Landing, Tennessee, April 6 & 7, 1862, I have to state that: Everett Peabody, Colonel of the 25th Mo. Vol. Inft., was in command of the first Brigade 6th Division and I was senior

Captain of the regiment.

At early morn before breakfast the line of Battle was formed, with the right of Brigade resting on the right of our regimental colour line. My company was on the right of Brigade. A few minutes after the line was formed, General Prentiss rode up near Colonel Peabody, who was mounted and in front of my company, about the centre of the first platoon and said to him, "Colonel Peabody, I hold you responsible for bringing on this fight."

Saluting, Colonel Peabody said: "If I brought on the fight I am able to lead the van." General Prentiss ordered him to take his best regiment . . . . the next words I heard were: "25th Missouri, forward."

Signed   Yours respectfully,

F. C. Nichols,

Captain U. S. Army, Retired;

formerly Major & Capt. 25th Mo.

Vol. Inf. War of '61 & 5.

This letter by Capt. Nichols makes clear and positive two important points: (1) that General Prentiss, like General Sherman, was impressed with the idea that, under General Halleck's orders the enemy was to be avoided rather than sought out, and he reprimanded his brigade commander for doing, irregularly, the very thing that saved the army from the "surprise" about which so many untruths have been told; (2) the letter makes it clear that Prentiss's division was neither in bed nor at breakfast, when the attack came—it was in line "before breakfast", and the enemy was received with a hot fire, as will appear.

Prentiss's reprimand of Colonel Peabody was, doubtless, prompted by the same sense of responsibility as was that administered by General Sherman to Colonel Buckland, already mentioned. It had been "ground into" each division commander, so to speak, that, "in no case" were they "to be drawn into an engagement."

There was another incident in the activities immediately preceding the battle, more important than anything yet mentioned, which, however, was not revealed, until forty years later—an incident which, had it been known when and by whom it should have been known, the Battle of Shiloh would have had a different story to tell. We now know, though the knowledge is comparatively recent but entirely reliable, that General Lew. Wallace, commanding the second division of the army at Crump's Landing, had positive information of the movement of the Confederate army to attack Grant on the very day that the movement began—information brought directly to him by one trusted scout and confirmed by a second. During two full days and three nights ("for three days and nights," to quote his language) he "simmers" this all-important information in his mind, trying to determine how he could best re-enforce the comrades beyond Snake Creek in case of need.

General Wallace tells in his *Autobiography* how and when the information came to him of the movement of the Confederate army from Corinth as follows:

> About as the sun set, Thursday, the 4th [3rd], Bell the scout came into my tent, evidently the worse for a hard ride, and said, abruptly, 'I bring you news, sir. . . . The whole rebel army is on the way up from Corinth. . . . They set out this morning early. By this time they are all on the road . . . . batteries and all.' This important information was confirmed by another scout (Carpenter): 'Johnston's cut loose and is making for Pittsburg.' [41]

General Wallace says that he sent this information by his orderly, on the same evening to Pittsburg Landing, with instructions in case Grant was not found to leave the dispatch with the postmaster, to be delivered next morning. General Wallace's excuse for not sending a proper officer with positive orders to find Grant, seems almost too puerile to be credited—he did not want to appear "officious". The dispatch never reached its proper destination, and the secret was in the keeping of General Wallace until he disclosed it in his *Autobiography*. For his own reputation, it might better have died with him.

A dispatch boat was at all times at Wallace's headquarters, subject to his orders, and there should have been no difficulty in the way of finding General Grant within two hours, whether at the Landing above or at Savannah below. It is worth remembering in this connection that the orderly sent with this dispatch went by the river road and over Snake Creek bridge which had been repaired on that very day under direction of Colonel McPherson, Halleck's chief engineer. General Wallace pleaded ignorance of this road, two days later, in excusing himself for marching his division over the wrong road.

THE UNION ARMY AND THE FIELD

To understand and properly appreciate the difficulties under which

---

41 Wallace's *Autobiography*, Vol. 1, pp. 454–456.

the Battle of Shiloh was fought on the Union side, the composition of the Army and the topography of the field must both be considered. The Army of the Tennessee as it was camped in the woods above Pittsburg Landing on Sunday morning, April 6, 1862, was never in a camp of organization and instruction, as an Army—it grew by accretion, beginning at Fort Donelson in the middle of February preceding. Some of the regiments that stormed the enemy's works at Donelson dropped into line for the first time under fire, and only a few hours before the assault was made.

In like manner new and untrained regiments and batteries came, one by one, to swell the ranks at Shiloh, even after the roar of battle sounded through the woods, taking their assigned places under fire. The division (Prentiss's 6th) from which the reconnoitring party went out before daylight on Sunday morning to "surprise" the enemy was the newest of the new, having but two organized brigades—though there was enough "raw material" assigned to the division for a third brigade, not all on the ground, however, when the battle began. Attention is called to these facts for the reason that they should be taken into account in passing judgment upon the Battle of Shiloh.

Besides the lack of organization and drill of the army the character of the field upon which the battle was fought should be considered. It has been said with much truth that a clear understanding of the Battle of Shiloh cannot be had without studying the movements on the ground. A written description can convey only a very general idea of the plateau upon which the battle was fought; hence a map showing the principal streams, roads, open fields, etc., is added to aid the study of the positions and movements (Map 2).

The plateau, rising eighty to one hundred feet above the Tennessee on the east, was surrounded by almost impassable barriers on all sides—except an opening to the southwest, two and a half to three miles in width. The plateau sheds its waters west, north, and east— west and northwest into Owl Creek; north into Snake Creek; and east into the Tennessee. The creeks were effectually guarded by swampy margins and heavy timber, or by a combination of the three—timber, under-brush, and swamp. They admitted of no crossing except by bridges, of which there was one on each of the streams leading to and from the battle field. The Tennessee could be crossed only by boat, as the army had never been supplied with pontoons.

This plateau, bordered as described, was cut into numerous gullies and ravines by small spring-branches, running to all points of the compass in finding their tortuous ways to the larger streams. Most of these spring-branches ran through marshy ground—impassable in the early spring except where bridged. Some of the ravines were deep, miry, and so densely choked with briers and brambles as to defy invasion by anything much larger than a rabbit. The hillsides and the ridges were covered with timber and underbrush, except where small farms were under cultivation. There was not an elevation anywhere on the three miles square from which a general view could be had. Wide flanking movements were impossible to either army, and cavalry was practically useless.

The Landing itself was a mud bank at the foot of a steep bluff, a single road winding around the bluff and up the hillside to higher ground. At a distance of about a half-mile from the Landing the road forked and a little further on struck the Hamburg and Savannah road, running nearly parallel with the river. Still further on the Corinth road crossed the Hamburg and Purely road and struck the Bark road, one branch three miles out and the other branch four miles out. Besides these main roads shown on the map, there were numerous farm roads winding around on the ridges, and the needs of the army made many new roads—all were deep in mud made of the most tenacious clay, so that the unloading of boats and the hauling to camp was a slow and laborious process for both man and mule.

Had John Codman Ropes understood the topography and other conditions of the field of Shiloh, he would hardly have ventured to criticise General Johnston for making a front attack upon the commands of Hurlbut, Prentiss, and Wallace, and for failing to force his way along the Hamburg and Savannah road on the Union left at an earlier hour. General Johnston had no choice but to make a front attack and he did his best to force his way along the Hamburg and Savannah road, toward the Landing at the earliest possible hour. Why and how he failed to accomplish his main object, before the close of the day, will appear later. The ground between the Hamburg and Savannah road and the river was much broken—so much so that there were but two or three cultivated fields on that part of the plateau.

THE CONFEDERATE ARMY AND ITS OBJECTIVE

As already stated, after the surrender of Fort Donelson and the evacuation of Nashville General Johnston's army fell back as rapidly as possible southward to the line of the Memphis and Charleston Railroad with a view to joining General Beauregard, who commanded the territory west of the Tennessee River with headquarters at Corinth. By the last week in March there had been concentrated at Corinth and in the vicinity an army of 40,000 effective men, and General Johnston took command on the 29th of March with General Beauregard second in command.

The object to be accomplished by this army was to attack and defeat Grant's army before the arrival of Buell, then on the march from Nashville with 37,000 men, following up this anticipated success with the defeat of Buell, thus opening the way back to Nashville so recently evacuated. The movement from Corinth and surrounding camps to attack Grant began in the early morning of April 3rd, with a view to making the attack early on the 5th. Bad weather and bad roads delayed the attack twenty-four hours—to Sunday morning, April 6th. How the expected "surprise" of Grant's army was anticipated will now be told.

THE BATTLE

It is not the purpose to describe in detail the movements of the battle throughout the two days, but only to touch upon salient features. One of the salient features, and not the least important, is that of the action of the reconnoitring party heretofore referred to as having been sent out before daylight on Sunday morning from Prentiss's division. General Prentiss in his official report makes no mention of the Powell party, but he says that "at 3 o'clock ... Col. David Moore, Twenty-first Missouri, with five companies of his infantry regiment, proceeded to the front, and at break of day the advance pickets were driven in". [42]

Colonel Moore, in his official report, says that he was ordered out by Colonel Peabody, commanding the First Brigade, "at about 6 o'clock", to support the picket guard which "had been attacked and driven in". It appears to be certain, therefore, that both the reconnoitring party under Major Powell and the support under Colonel Moore were ordered out by Colonel Peabody without consulting the division commander; hence the reprimand above quoted—heard and remembered by many others besides Captain Nichols. Colonel Moore's command was a re-enforcing not a reconnoitring party.

The line of march of the Powell party may be traced on the map (No. 2) along the road passing the camp of the 25th Missouri, past the southeast corner of Rhea Field and the north side of Seay Field, pass-

---

42 *War of the Rebellion*: Official Records, Series 1, Vol. 10, Part 1, p. 278.

ing the picket line at the forks of the road and striking the corner of Fraley Field a few rods farther on. From this point the *videttes* of the Confederate picket, under Major Hardcastle of Hardee's corps were encountered. The *videttes* fired upon the advancing party and retired to the picket line at the southwest corner of Fraley Field. The fight between the picket post and Powell's party began at once, though it was still quite dark—"too dark to see, in the timber and underbrush", so the firing at first was at random.

As there never was an official report made of the part taken by the Powell reconnoitring party, as both the officer ordering it out and the officer commanding it were killed early in the main battle, we must rely upon the report of the officer commanding the Confederate picket at Fraley Field for the incidents of that encounter. Major Hardcastle says the firing began "about dawn" (at 4:55 in fact), and he says: "We fought the enemy an hour or more without giving an inch". "At about 6:30" he saw the brigade formed behind him and "fell back". The casualties in Major Hardcastle's command were four killed and nineteen wounded. [43] The casualties in the Powell party were never certainly known.

This stubborn picket fight seems to have been something of a "surprise" to at least one of the Confederate generals. General Bragg, commanding the second line of attack, says in his official report that "the enemy did not give us time to discuss the question of attack, for soon after dawn he commenced a rapid musketry fire on our pickets." [44] Major Hardcastle, commanding this picket line, says: "The enemy opened a heavy fire on us at a distance of about two hundred yards". [45] That the Confederate line was not ready to move forward at once when the firing began appears from Major Hardcastle's official report. He says: "At about 6:30 a. m. I saw the brigade formed in my rear and fell back." [45]

So there was a full hour and a half elapsed between the beginning of the firing and the movement forward. The battle front, two and a half to three miles in extent with a curtain of skirmishers, advanced to the attack. Major Powell's party and the Union pickets that joined him fell slowly back, carrying their dead and wounded until they met Colonel Moore with five companies of his regiment (21st Missouri). Colonel Moore taking command, sent back for the other five compa-

43 *War of the Rebellion*: Official Records, Series 1, Vol. 10, Part 1, p. 603.
44 *War of the Rebellion*: Official Records, Series 1, Vol. 10, Part 1, p. 464.
45 *War of the Rebellion*: Official Records, Series 1, Vol. 10, Part 1, p. 603.

nies of his regiment, under Lieutenant Colonel Woodyard.

The force now consisted of the 21st Missouri, three companies of the 25th Missouri, four companies of the 16th Wisconsin, and two companies of the 12th Michigan—all infantry. This force formed in Seay Field and advanced to a point near the northwest corner of the field, where the Confederate skirmishers were encountered, the 8th and 9th Arkansas (Map 3). There was a sharp fight at this point lasting about thirty minutes, in which Colonel Moore was severely wounded. Lieutenant Mann of the same regiment was wounded, and Captain Saxe (16th Wisconsin) was killed—the first Union officer killed in the Battle of Shiloh.

As the Confederates advanced, the little Union force moved slowly back across Shiloh Branch, forming again at a point about two hundred yards from the southeast corner of Rhea Field, where the remainder of Peabody's brigade was in line. This position was held from a half hour to an hour against two brigades (Shaver's and Wood's). While falling back in line from this point Major King (21st Missouri) was mortally wounded. Meantime, General Prentiss had formed the remainder of his division (Miller's brigade) and had advanced about eighty rods from the front of his camp to the south side of Spain Field (Map 3), where he was joined by Peabody's brigade, Powell's party, and the pickets.

The division, now consisting of seven regiments and two batteries, was here attacked by four brigades—Wood, Shaver, Gladden, and Chalmers—comprising twenty regiments and three batteries. Against this tremendous odds the position was held for about thirty minutes, when the division fell back to the line of the camp where another stand of about thirty minutes was made, the division finally retiring at about nine o'clock—more than five hours after the reconnoitring party marched out. Among the casualties on the Union side in front of Prentiss's division were Colonel Peabody and Major Powell, killed [46]; and on the Confederate side General Gladden was mortally wounded.

There is ample testimony in the official reports of Confederate officers to show that the resistance met by their several commands in the slow advance from the picket line had none of the features of a sham battle. There were many casualties on both sides—how many

---

46 Since writing the above the author has learned from General Charles Morton, who helped to carry the body from the field, that Major Powell was killed later in the day—about noon, at the Hornets' Nest.

was never certainly known. There was no bayoneting of Union men on their beds in their tents or elsewhere. Indeed there was never any foundation for such stories except in the imagination of sensational newspaper correspondents. And it is further to be stated that at the time when the lines came in collision at the front—about 8 o'clock— every regiment in the camp, three miles in extent, was in line waiting orders or was marching toward the sound of battle.

A word of explanation should here be made in regard to General Sherman's (5th) division. This division was the first to go into camp at Pittsburg Landing, and the necessities of the situation required it to cover three important approaches from the back country to the Landing; namely, the main Corinth road; a bridge on the Hamburg and Purdy road over Owl Creek; and a ford over Lick Creek near its mouth which accommodated travel from Hamburg both to Purdy and Savannah.

The crossing of Owl Creek was about three miles west of the Landing, and the crossing of Lick Creek was about the same distance to the south of the Landing; while the Corinth road ran southwest nearly midway between the two crossings. General Sherman camped three brigades (1st, 3rd, and 4th) to occupy the Corinth road at Shiloh meeting-house, thus covering Owl Creek bridge. The other brigade (Stuart's) camping to cover Lick Creek crossing, was separated from the division by a little more than one mile, and it remained separated throughout the first day's battle, acting independently of the orders of the division commander.

The space between the two parts of Sherman's division was later occupied by General Prentiss's (6th) division formed of new regiments as they arrived. When reference is hereafter made to Sherman's division, in the action of Sunday, it is to be understood that Stuart's brigade is not included for the reasons explained.

Still another explanation is needed. When General Sherman first went into camp special attention was paid to the selection of camping sites convenient to good water. By consulting the map it will be seen that three brigades of this division were camped somewhat irregularly, the left brigade being out of line with the other brigades and also out of line in itself. As a consequence when line of battle was formed on Sunday morning it was not a prolonged line, the left of Hildebrand's brigade being well forward and in an open field where it was peculiarly exposed to the force of the first onset to which it quickly yielded as will be seen.

At a little after seven o'clock, and after line of battle had been formed, General Sherman and staff rode to the left of his division in Rhea Field for a better view to the front; and while there in front of the 53rd Ohio regiment (Colonel Appier) the Confederate skirmishers opened fire from the brush across Shiloh Branch, killing the general's orderly.

At about eight o'clock, looking off to the "left front", there were seen "the glistening bayonets of masses of infantry", and then, for the first time, General Sherman was convinced that "the enemy designed a determined attack." [47] A few minutes later the Confederate advance struck Sherman's left under Colonel Hildebrand, and Prentiss's right under Colonel Peabody. How Prentiss's division met the attack has already been stated. How Sherman's division met it will now be shown.

The 53rd Ohio, exposed as has been explained, and commanded, unfortunately, by an officer whose nerve deserted him at the critical moment, after firing two volleys, became demoralized and as an organization disappeared, though two companies were rallied by their officers, joined other organizations and staid on the firing line throughout the day. Colonel Appier disappeared from the field and was later cashiered for cowardice.

The attack on Sherman's left and centre by Cleburne's brigade of Hardee's corps was furious and sustained—to be repulsed, however, with heavy loss, by Buckland's brigade and the two remaining regiments of Hildebrand's brigade. Cleburne, in his official report of this affair, says: "Everywhere his musketry and artillery at short range swept the open spaces with an iron storm that threatened certain destruction to every living thing that would dare to cross them Under the terrible fire much confusion followed, and a quick and bloody repulse was the consequence." [48]

One of Cleburne's regiments (6th Miss.) lost three hundred men, killed and wounded, out of 425, and his brigade soon went to pieces. A second assault was made by Anderson's brigade of Bragg's corps to meet a similar repulse. A third assault was made by two brigades of Polk's corps (Russell's and Johnson's) joined with the reorganized brigades of Cleburne and Anderson and assisted by Wood on their right. This assault was successful, forcing Sherman from his first line at about ten o'clock, and with him one brigade of McClernand's division that

---

47 *War of the Rebellion*: Official Records, Series 1, Vol. 10, Part 1I, p. 294.
48 *War of the Rebellion*: Official Records, Series 1, Vol. 10, Part 1, p. 581.

had come to his support on the left.

Sherman's right brigade (McDowell's) was not involved in this engagement for the reason that the line of attack crossed its front diagonally without bringing it into action; but a little later Pond's brigade, from the extreme left of Bragg's corps, appeared in McDowell's front, overlapping his right and covering Owl Creek bridge. Orders were then given to fall back to the Purdy road, and McDowell's camp was abandoned without a fight.

By this tune Hildebrand's brigade had gone to pieces and Hildebrand himself being without a command, reported to General McClernand for staff duty. In fact this first assault on Sherman's line fell mainly upon a single brigade (Buckland's), and it was on the hillside in his front where, according to General Lew. Wallace, there was "a pavement of dead men", after the fight was over. This must be considered one of the conspicuous features of Sunday's battle. Time was of the utmost importance, to enable the proper formations in distant parts of the camp. The needed time was secured by the stubborn fight made by Sherman's division on its first line; and it was probably this that gained for General Sherman, in the minds of some, credit for saving the day.

It was in the Confederate plan to push its right east to the river, turn the Union left, seize the Landing, and force the army back on Owl Creek where it was expected surrender would necessarily follow. The stubbornness of the resistance to the Confederate left delayed the movement toward the river somewhat, though two brigades (Chalmers's and Jackson's) were in front of the Union left near the mouth of Lick Creek, very soon after the extreme right fell back from the first line. To meet these two brigades of nine regiments and two batteries, Colonel Stuart had a single brigade of three regiments without artillery—and one of these regiments (71st Ohio) was led off the field by its colonel soon after the fight began, to take no further part in the day's battle. Colonel Mason was later cashiered for his conduct at Shiloh.

The two remaining regiments of this brigade gave a good account of themselves (55th Illinois and 54th Ohio), making heroic resistance and suffering severely in casualties. There are those who believe that the fighting on the extreme left by this little band of about eight hundred men without artillery and against three or four times their number with artillery was not less important than was the fighting on the extreme right, though less conspicuous. This movement of the

Confederate right was under the personal direction of General Johnston, and upon its quick success depended the success of the battle as planned. Before eleven o'clock the battle was raging from right to left, a distance of three to four miles.

As has been already stated, by the time that the battle was fairly on at the front every regiment in the most distant parts of the camp was in line. McClernand promptly supported Sherman, and Hurlbut also sent one of his brigades (Veatch's) to that part of the field, leading his two remaining brigades to support Prentiss. Hurlbut, meeting Prentiss's division falling back in disorder, allowed the men to drift through his ranks, then formed line at the Peach Orchard, facing Lauman's brigade west and Williams's brigade south, where he met first the attack of Chalmers's and Jackson's brigades from the direction of Prentiss's abandoned camp. A little later this position was attacked by the brigades of Bowen, Statham, Stephens, and Gladden—the latter officer, however, having received a mortal wound in front of Prentiss's first line, as already stated.

C. F. Smith's (2nd) division, now commanded by "W. H. L. Wallace, camped near the Landing, and fully three miles from the point where the battle began, was in line by eight o'clock, and the first brigade of four regiments (Colonel Tuttle) advanced to Duncan Field and took position in the "sunken road"—long abandoned as useless, but which ere nightfall was destined to become famous for desperate fighting against odds (Map 3). Of the second brigade (General McArthur's) one regiment was sent to the right; two were sent to cover Snake Creek bridge, over which General Lew. Wallace's division was expected at an early hour; and two marched under General McArthur himself, to the support of Stuart, on the extreme left.

The third brigade (Sweeny's) moved south on the Corinth road to act as a reserve, though it was not permitted to wait upon opportunity. Two regiments of this brigade (7th and 58th Illinois) were sent at once to the right to prolong Tuttle's line to connect with McClernand, going into position at about nine-thirty o 'clock. A third regiment (50th Illinois) was sent to McArthur on the left; and the remaining regiment of the brigade (8th Iowa), between eleven and twelve o 'clock, took position at Tuttle's left in the "sunken road" connecting its left with Prentiss who, having rallied a part of his division, put them in at the right of Hurlbut.

Prentiss was here joined under fire by the 23rd Missouri, just landed from the boats, giving him about one thousand men in the "Hornets' Nest". Two other regiments (15th and 16th Iowa), assigned to Prentiss's division, landing too late to join him at his camp, were sent to McClernand, joining him at Jones's Field, one and a half miles west of the Landing.

Before noon the contending armies were in continuous and compact line from flank to flank. Welded in the furnace heat of four hours' battle without a moment's respite, it might be said with little exaggeration that the men stood foot to foot, contending for the mastery. The Union lines had steadily but slowly receded, shortening at the flanks, and the Confederates had as steadily advanced, extending their flanks but recoiling again and again from attacks made at the centre, and with heavy loss.

The Confederate reserve under General Breckenridge, about 8,500 men, were all in action before noon, the first brigade (Trabue) going in on their extreme left at about the time that Sherman fell back from his first line. The other two brigades (Bowen and Statham) went into line on the right, south of the Peach Orchard, between eleven and twelve o'clock, in front of Hurlbut and near where General Johnston had his headquarters in the saddle. Though General Johnston personally directed the battle on the Confederate side, in this part of the field, he did not, as some writers have told the story, personally encourage an unwilling Tennessee regiment by riding along the line and tapping the bayonets of the men with a tin cup which he carried in his hand, then leading the line in a furious charge. No part of such an incident occurred there or elsewhere, on the authority of one of General Johnston's chief Aids, Governor Harris of Tennessee—the only person who was present at the death of General Johnston soon after, and near the spot where the incident is said to have occurred.

Stuart, McArthur, and Hurlbut having successfully repulsed several attacks, General Johnston was evidently convinced that the Union left was not to be easily turned; and so about noon under his personal direction, having put into his lines two brigades of the reserve under General Breckenridge, a forward movement was ordered, six brigades participating—Chalmers's, Jackson's, Bowen's, Statham's, Stephens's, and Gladden's. Threatened on his left by a cavalry flanking movement, Stuart was the first slowly to give ground; McArthur, on Stuart's right, necessarily followed, both changing front from south to southeast, falling back and fighting for every foot of ground.

This movement compelled Hurlbut to retire from his first position to the north side of the Peach Orchard (Map 4). At about two o'clock,

Colonel Stuart having been wounded, his two regiments having lost heavily, and having exhausted their ammunition—even after robbing the cartridge-boxes of their dead and wounded comrades—retired toward the Landing. General McArthur followed not long after; and General Hurlbut, having connected his right with General Prentiss's left, swung back until their lines were nearly at right angles (Map 5). Hurlbut retired toward the Landing at about four or four-thirty o'clock, leaving the line from left to right in the following order: Prentiss's command, 8th Iowa of Sweeny's brigade, Tuttle's full brigade, and the 58th Illinois of Sweeny's brigade.

While this fierce struggle was in progress on the Confederate right, at about two-thirty afternoon, General Johnston received the wound from which he died a few minutes later. General Bragg then took command of the right, and General Ruggles succeeded Bragg in the centre.

While the battle raged on the Union left, as described, it was not less stubborn and bloody on the right; but Sherman and McClernand were forced back to the Hamburg and Savannah road—a mile from the Landing—about four-thirty o'clock, the Confederates gradually closing in from both flanks around the centre (Map 6). Meantime General W. H. L. Wallace had sent orders for his command to retire; but for some reason never explained four of his six regiments did not receive the order and were captured, as will be explained. As General Wallace and General Tuttle, followed by the 2nd and 7th Iowa Regiments, were fighting their way through a severe crossfire at short range, General Wallace was mortally wounded, and was left on the field to be recovered the next day, dying three or four days later without recovering consciousness.

THE HORNETS' NEST

This appellation owes its origin to the men who felt the sting of the hornets. William Preston Johnston in his history of his father (General A. S. Johnston) speaks of the term as a "mild metaphor", and says that "no figure of speech would be too strong to express the deadly peril of an assault upon this natural fortress whose inaccessible barriers blazed for six hours with sheets of flame, and whose infernal gates poured forth a murderous storm of shot and shell and musket-fire which no living thing could quell or withstand". [49]

No more graphic description of the fight at the Hornets' Nest

---

49 Johnston's *Life of General A. S. Johnston*, p. 620.

has been written than that of which the language quoted is a part—written from the view-point of the attacking forces, and, therefore, written with full knowledge of the results that followed from the "murderous storm of shot and shell and musket-fire." It is literally true that Duncan Field and the woods and thickets bordering it along the "sunken road" were thickly strewn with the dead and wounded. The same author tells us that "Hindman's brilliant brigades .... were shivered into fragments and paralyzed"; that Stewart's regiments .... retired mangled from the field"; that "Gibson's splendid brigade .... recoiled and fell back"—four several times, indeed. Colonel Gibson, in his official report says of his brigade: "Four times the position was charged and four times the assault proved unavailing."

The best informed writer, living or dead, on the details and incidents of the Battle of Shiloh—Major D. W. Reed, Secretary and Historian of the Shiloh National Military Park Commission and author of *Campaigns and Battles Twelfth Regiment Iowa Veteran Volunteer Infantry*, who was himself in the Nest during the entire day, says there were "twelve separate and distinct charges" made upon the line at the Hornets' Nest, with the result that three Confederate brigades were "entirely disorganized", and that "thirteen regiments lost their regimental organizations .... and were not brought into the fight again .... during the day".[50] General Ruggles, who commanded the Confederate lines in that part of the field after the death of General Johnston, designates this as "one of the controlling conflicts of that eventful day."[51] The position was of such conspicuous importance that a brief description of the ground will not be out of place.

Moving out on the Corinth road from the Landing about three-fourths of a mile one crosses the Hamburg and Savannah road. A fourth of a mile further on the road forks, the left-hand branch (Eastern Corinth) bearing south of southwest; and one-fourth of a mile still further on it crosses an old abandoned road near the southeast corner of Duncan Field, and near the centre of the Hornets' Nest. The right-hand road from the fork runs nearly west, crossing the north end of Duncan Field, then bearing south passes the "Little Log Meetinghouse."

At the point where this road, going from the Landing, strikes the east line of Duncan Field the abandoned road leads off to the southeast about a half-mile, then bending east to the Hamburg and Savannah

50 Reed's *Campaigns and Battles of the Twelfth Regiment Iowa Veteran Volunteer Infantry*, p. 50.
51 *War of the Rebellion*: Official Records, Series 1, Vol. 10, Part 1, p. 475.

road near Bloody Pond—another significant local name. Along this abandoned road, beginning near the north end of Duncan Field, the line of battle from right to left, was as follows: 58th Illinois (Sweeny's brigade); second, seventh, twelfth, and fourteenth Iowa regiments (Tuttle's brigade); to the left of this brigade was the eighth Iowa, of Sweeny's brigade; to the left still was Prentiss's division, consisting of one entire regiment (23rd Missouri), and parts of several other regiments—the entire line numbering not to exceed 2,500 men.

The old road ran along a slight elevation and was so water-washed in places as to afford good shelter to men lying down to fire on an advancing enemy—a sort of natural rifle-pit, though rather shallow in places. About half of the distance, from right to left, there was open field extending to the front about 500 yards to the timber occupied by the Confederates. The left half of the line was well screened by timber and, for the most part, by a heavy growth of underbrush so that the advancing lines not able to see the men lying in the old road were received with a crushing fire at short range. In every instance the repulse was complete and bloody.

General Ruggles, becoming convinced that the position could not be taken by infantry, from the front, determined to concentrate his artillery and bombard the strong-hold. He tells us in his official report[52] that he directed his staff officers "to bring forward all the field guns they could collect from the left toward the right". General Ruggles evidently believed that this was a crisis in the battle, admitting that "for a brief period the enemy apparently gained". Nor was he alone in the belief, for one of his artillery officers (Captain Sandidge) said officially: "I have no doubt that had they been seasonably reinforced when they checked our advancing troops, they could certainly have broken our lines."

And he feared that result before the guns could be planted and infantry supports brought up. General Ruggles succeeded in bringing up sixty-two guns from the left, which were planted on the west side of Duncan Field about five hundred yards away; and the bombardment began at about four-thirty afternoon. Of course there could be but one result. The Union batteries were forced to retire, leaving the way clear for the encircling Confederate lines to close in. Besides the Ruggles aggregation of artillery of sixty-two guns, there must have been several other batteries playing upon the Hornets' Nest from the

---

52 *War of the Rebellion*: Official Records, Series 1, Vol. 10, Part 1, p. 472.

right, as none of the guns from that part of the field were in the Ruggles aggregation. Probably not less than seventy-five guns were trained on that devoted spot, and fully three-fourths of the Confederate army was coiling around it.

And for some time before the surrender took place, a few minutes before six o'clock, rifle-fire poured in from three directions, as the beleaguered faced about and attempted to fight their way out, The number to surrender was about 2,000 men. The importance of this prolonged contest, from a little before ten forenoon to nearly six afternoon, upon the destinies of the day can hardly be estimated. It secured to General Grant's army the thing most needed—time to form the new line; time for Lew. Wallace, for Buell, and for Night to come. The Hornets' Nest was distinctly an altar of sacrifice (Map 6).

How Buell Saved the Day

By the time the Confederate officers had recovered from their "surprise" at the smallness of the capture at the Hornets' Nest, in view of the prolonged and effective resistance encountered, General Grant had formed his new line on the north side of Dill Branch, running from the mouth of the Branch on a curve back to the road leading from the Landing; thence west to the Hamburg and Savannah road; thence north to the swamp bordering Snake Creek.

At the extreme left of the line, the two gunboats lay opposite the mouth of the Branch. On the bluffs near the mouth of the Branch were two batteries, trained up-stream. Two other batteries were a little farther from the river and back nearer the road leading from the Landing; and two more were still farther west, but advanced toward the edge of the bluffs overlooking the Branch. Back on the road again and a little west were two more batteries before coming to the six big siege guns.

A glance at the map for Sunday night's position will show that the line from the mouth of Dill Branch west to the siege guns was a semicircle with the gunboats at the extreme left, and that there were about fifty guns in the line east of the Hamburg and Savannah road, exclusive of the gunboats. Behind this array of artillery was ample infantry support, except on the extreme left where support was not needed, because of the nature of the ground in front.

As General Nelson marched the head of his column up from the Landing at about five-thirty o'clock, he noted the absence of infantry along that part of the line, and in his official report he describes what he saw as a "semicircle of artillery, totally unsupported by infantry", which was not quite true; and he added another statement which was not at all true, namely; "the left of the artillery was completely turned by the enemy and the gunners fled from their pieces." [53] General Nelson evidently knew nothing of the batteries near the mouth of Dill Branch, for he struck the line at about the middle of the "semicircle" and the single regiment that he brought into action (36th Indiana) was sent to support the guns in front of the main line toward Dill Branch.

Opposed to this array of Union artillery a single Confederate battery took part in the last attack, and that was disabled.

Any fair-minded person, having knowledge of the character of the ground between the lines of the two armies as the lines were on Sunday night—especially on the left of the Union lines—must admit that Grant's was a strong position and that his antagonist had serious obstacles to overcome before he could strike with effect.

With as little delay as possible after the surrender at the Hornets' Nest, General Bragg, still commanding the Confederate right, ordered his division commanders to "drive the enemy into the river", believing, doubtless, that the "drive" would be a brief and easy task. Accordingly the Confederate right uncoiled itself from around the Hornets' Nest and, led by Chalmers's and Jackson's brigades of Withers's division, advanced along the road toward the Landing; then, filing right, formed line on the south side of Dill Branch and near the margin of the deep ravine. This ravine, impassable at its mouth by reason of steep bluffs and backwater, was difficult to pass fully a half-mile from its mouth. Its steep sides were timbered and obstructed by underbrush, and at the bottom it was fairly choked with undergrowth.

The last attack made upon the Union lines was upon the extreme left in which only two small brigades and one battery participated. Chalmers's brigade had nominally five regiments, but one of the regiments (52nd Tennessee) "acted badly" in the early part of the day, and three hundred of its four hundred men are not to be counted. Jackson's brigade detached one regiment to guard the Hornets' Nest prisoners, so that it seems to be liberal, allowing for the losses of the day, to say that there were not to exceed 1800 men engaged in the last assault.

The two brigades made their way down the southern slope, through the tangled undergrowth at the bottom of the ravine and, quoting

---

53 *War of the Rebellion: Official Records*, Series 1, Vol. 10, Part 1, p. 323.

from their official reports, "struggled" up the other slope, "which was very steep" encountering in "attempting to mount the last ridge" the "fire from a whole line of batteries protected by infantry and assisted by shells from the gunboats." General Chalmers says his men "were too much exhausted to storm the batteries". [54]

General Jackson says his men were without ammunition, having "only their bayonets to rely on", and that when "they arrived near the crest of the opposite hill", they "could not be urged farther without support", the men "sheltering themselves against the precipitous sides of the ravine" where "they remained under fire for some time." [55] (The Confederate skirmish line is shown on Map 6, at the crest of the bluff, north of Dill Branch.)

This was the situation when eight companies of the 36th Indiana (Colonel Grose), about four hundred men, of Ammen's brigade, Nelson's division, Army of the Ohio, arrived on the scene. Colonel Grose was ordered to go to the support of Stone's battery, which was in position some distance in advance of Grant's main line and near the brow of the hill up which the assailants were climbing with great difficulty. There the 36th Indiana exchanged shots with the skirmishers of Chalmers's brigade, during fifteen to thirty minutes [56] having one man killed and one man wounded. In his history of the 36th Indiana, Colonel Grose says that "after three or four rounds the enemy fell back. It was then dark." And he says, further, that "no part of Buell's army, except the Thirty-sixth Indiana, took any part whatever in the Sunday evening fight at Shiloh."

And he might have said with equal truth and without disparagement to his regiment that the presence of the Thirty-sixth Indiana had no effect in determining the issues of the day. Had the four hundred men not been there the "enemy" would have retired just the same, for he could never have crossed the open space from the "last ridge" to the "line of batteries". The ground to be traversed was but gently rolling with little to obstruct the view—no sheltering ridge or friendly copse to admit of unobserved approach. It must have been a "rush" of two to four hundred yards, in the face of point-blank firing, to reach the batteries, behind which, as already stated, was ample infantry support. The battle of the day really came to an end at the Hornets' Nest. All that followed was mere skirmishing for the purpose of developing

54 *War of the Rebellion*: Official Records, Series 1, Vol. 10, Part 1, pp. 550-551.
55 *War of the Rebellion*: Official Records, Series 1, Vol. 10, Part 1, p. 555.
56 *War of the Rebellion*: Official Records, Series 1, Vol. 10, Part 1, p. 334.

the new conditions.

THE LOST OPPORTUNITY

The "Lost Opportunity" is a phrase of Confederate origin and it refers to the last moments of Sunday's battle, briefly described above. Both the idea and the phrase seem to have been born of an after-thought, and a disposition to shift blame to the shoulders of General Beauregard, should blame be imputed, for failure to crush or capture Grant's army. The claim has been put forward with considerable per-sistency that the order of General Beauregard to withdraw from the contest was responsible for the escape of Grant's army. This absurd claim has been answered most effectively by General Thomas Jordan, Adjutant-General of the Confederate forces engaged at Shiloh.

In *Southern Historical Society Papers*, [57] General Jordan takes up the subject and refers to the official reports of several division, brigade, and regimental commanders for the purpose of showing the demoralized and exhausted condition of the Confederate army. In referring to the report of General Withers, two brigades of whose division made the last feeble assault, he says:

> If there be significance in words, he makes it clear that such was the absolute lateness of the hour, that had the attempt been made to carry the Federal batteries .... with such troops as were there assembled, it would have resulted in an awful butchery and dispersion of all employed in so insensate, so preposterous an undertaking; and such must be the verdict of any military man who may studiously read the reports of the subordinate officers of Withers's three brigades, and bear in mind the for-midable line of fifty-odd pieces of artillery which Webster had improvised.[58]

Surgeon J. C. Nott of General Bragg's staff, who rode by his chief's side nearly all day, is quoted as saying that the

> men .... were too much demoralized and indisposed to advance in the face of the shells .... bursting over us in every direction, and my impression was .... that our troops had done all that they would do, and had better be withdrawn.[59]

Another officer of General Bragg's staff, Colonel Urquhart, writ-

---

57 *Southern Historical Society Papers*, Vol. 16, p. 297.
58 *Southern Historical Society Papers*, Vol. 16, pp. 300, 301.
59 *Southern Historical Society Papers*, Vol. 16, p. 307.

ing in 1880 is quoted thus:

> The plain truth must be told, that our troops at the front were a thin line of exhausted men, who were making no further headway Several years of subsequent service have impressed me that General Beauregard's order for withdrawing the troops was most timely. [60]

The claim that there was a "Lost Opportunity" because of the order to retire, General Jordan says, "becomes simply shameful, under the light of the closely contemporaneous statements of every division commander, except one (Withers); of all the brigade and regimental commanders of each Confederate corps, including the reserve whose reports have reached the light; that is, of nearly all commanders present in the battle." [61]

This ought to be sufficient evidence to settle forever both propositions in the negative; namely, the claim that Buell "saved the day", and that there was a "Lost Opportunity".

The condition of Grant's army at the close of Sunday's battle as to strength has been greatly underrated by certain writers, and its disorganization has been greatly exaggerated by writers who have had an object in so representing it. It is true that both armies were badly battered as the result of about fourteen hours' continuous fighting with scarcely a moment's cessation. Careful study of the reports of Confederate officers shows that there was not a single point of attack on any part of the field at any hour of the day where there was not stubborn resistance with serious loss to the attacking forces.

These reports also show that there was serious defection from their ranks, beginning early and continuing during the day, and that when night came on there was such disorganization that some of their commanders were entirely separated from their commands and remained so separated to the close of the battle, Monday night. These reports further show that instead of bivouacking in line of battle as did Grant's army the entire Confederate army, with the exception of a single brigade (Pond's brigade on the extreme left) withdrew a distance of two to four miles from the Landing.

It is in evidence also from the same sources of information that General Beauregard was able to put in line on the morning of the second day substantially half the number of men that were in line on

---

60 *Southern Historical Society Papers,* Vol. 16, p. 316.
61 *Southern Historical Society Papers,* Vol. 16, pp. 316317.

the morning of the first day. General Grant was able to put in line about the same proportion, exclusive of the reinforcements that came up during the night.

There are no means of determining the comparative casualties in the two armies on the first day, but there is no reason for doubting that they were substantially equal—exclusive of the capture at the Hornets' Nest. It is known, however, that the casualties among field officers, from the grade of colonel upward, were greater in the Union than in the Confederate army in Sunday's battle.

Much has been said about the "stragglers" from the Union lines crowding the Landing and "cowering" under the river bluffs—and with about the same degree of exaggeration as certain writers have indulged in their descriptions of the opening of the battle. There were "stragglers" from both armies, and there is no reason to doubt that the numbers were substantially equal. It is true, however, that the straggling was more in evidence on the Union side, for the very good reason that it was more concentrated—confined to a limited area about the Landing—while on the other side there was unlimited room for expansion and scattering over miles of territory.

This remark applies with equal force to other features of the crowded condition near the Landing, late in the day. Hundreds of teamsters with their four-mule and six-mule teams were there because it was the only place of safety for one of the essential parts of the army's equipment; the sick from the regimental hospitals and company tents were there—several hundred of them—because there was no other place to go; and hundreds of wounded were there from the front, together with a force of hospital attendants. Add these together and you have several thousand without counting a single "straggler". These things are never considered by critics who have a cause to support. Every large army requires a small army to care for it, who are, necessarily, non-combatants.

BUELL COMES ON THE FIELD

By General Orders of March 31st, General Grant's headquarters were transferred from Savannah to Pittsburg Landing; but a headquarters' office was continued at the former place for convenience up to the day of the battle, and General Grant passed between the two places every day, or nearly every day, on the headquarters' boat, *Tigress*. On Sunday morning, at Savannah, an "early breakfast" had been ordered, as it was General Grant's purpose to ride out with his staff to meet General Buell, whose arrival the evening before was not known. While at breakfast, firing was heard in the direction of Pittsburg Landing—"the breakfast was left unfinished" and General Grant and staff went directly to the boat and steamed rapidly up the river, stopping at Crump's Landing to order General Lew. Wallace to hold his division in readiness for marching orders.

Before leaving Savannah General Grant sent to General Nelson of Buell's army, the following order:

An attack having been made on our forces, you will move your entire command to the river opposite Pittsburg. [62]

A similar order was sent to General Wood, commanding another division of Buell's army, not yet arrived at Savannah, to move "with the utmost dispatch to the river" at Savannah, where boats would meet him. The following note was left for General Buell whose presence in Savannah was not known to General Grant:

Savannah, April 6, 1862

General D. C. Buell:

Heavy firing is heard up the river, indicating plainly that an attack has been made on our most advanced positions. I have been looking for this, but did not believe that the attack could be made before Monday or Tuesday. This necessitates my joining the forces up the river instead of meeting you today, as I had contemplated. I have directed General Nelson to move to the river with his division. He can march to opposite Pittsburg.

Respectfully, your obedient servant,

U. S. Grant

Major-General Commanding. [63]

This note clearly shows that General Grant, in common with his division commanders, was expecting an early attack.

As soon as General Grant, after arriving on the field, learned the true situation, he sent a staff officer with another order to General Nelson:

You will hurry up your command as fast as possible. All looks well but it is necessary for you to push forward as fast as possible. [64]

---

62 *War of the Rebellion*: Official Records, Series 1, Vol. 10, Part 2, p. 95.
63 *War of the Rebellion*; Official Records, Vol. 52, Part 1, p. 232.
64 *War of the Rebellion*: Official Records, Series 1, Vol. 10, Part 2, pp. 95-96.

Later still, probably about noon though it may have been later, nothing having been heard either from Buell or Nelson, General Grant sent another hurry-up order addressed to the "Commanding Officer Advance Forces (Buell's Army)". This order was delivered to General Buell on the boat as he was going to the Landing. He arrived at the Landing, he tells us in *Shiloh Reviewed*, about 1 o'clock, though Villard, who claims to have been on the same boat, makes the time later, between 5 and 6 o'clock, about the time that Nelson's advance crossed the river. And there are certain features of Buell's official report which, in the absence of a definite statement on the point, make Villard's claim as to the hour at least plausible.

General Grant's first order to General Nelson must have been received as early as 7 o'clock—probably earlier, for Nelson had the order when General Buell, after hearing the firing, went to General Grant's headquarters for information, where he learned that the latter had "just started for the Landing". [65]

General Nelson in his official report does not state the hour of receiving the order to march, but says that he "left Savannah, by order of General Grant, reiterated by General Buell in person, at 1.30 p. m." [66] The language is a little ambiguous, but it doubtless means that the order was "reiterated" about noon or later and that the march began at one-thirty, afternoon.[67] (Colonel Ammen says at one, afternoon.)

Villard, heretofore quoted, says that Nelson received Grant's order about noon, by which he probably means the "reiterated" order. In any event it appears that General Buell "held up" the order to Nelson fully five hours and then "reiterated" it. Why did General Buell do that? Why did General Nelson wait to have the order "reiterated"? Why did he not obey the original order regardless of any dilatory order from General Buell, since the contingency had arisen under which by General Halleck's instructions General Grant was "authorized to take the general command" of both armies; namely, an attack upon his own army? Had General Nelson marched under the original order, his division would have been on the field at about the time that it started on the ten-mile march. What might have been the effect of throwing 4,500 fresh men in the scale of battle, then hanging in doubtful poise, is, of course, conjectural—and it must be left to conjecture, though there is little room for doubt.

65 *War of the Rebellion*: Official Records, Series 1, Vol. 10, Part 1. p. 292.
66 *War of the Rebellion*: Official Records, Series 1, Vol. 10, Part 1, p. 323.
67 *War of the Rebellion*: Official Records, Series 1, Vol. 10, Part 1, p. 323.

General Nelson's entire division was across the river soon after dark. Advancing a little to the front on the extreme left it bivouacked for the night. A little later General Lew. Wallace came up on the extreme right, his division numbering about 5,000 men; but having to counter-march the division in order to bring the regiments in proper position his formation was not completed until after midnight when it went into bivouac.

During Sunday night Crittenden's division of Buell's army (two brigades) came up by boat, and in the morning two brigades of Mc-Cook's division arrived, to be joined about noon by another brigade. Wood's division, which was about thirty miles away when the battle began, arrived on the field at about two afternoon Monday, when the battle was about over. The total additions to the Union lines up to noon on Monday was approximately 20,000 men.

During Sunday's battle General Grant passed from point to point behind the firing line, meeting and consulting with his division commanders and carefully observing the movements of the contending forces, for, as has already been stated, there was no point on the field from which general observations could be made. On Monday he commanded his own army, giving no orders to General Buell, the latter exercising independent command. Why General Grant did not assume "general command" of both armies we might fairly conjecture (if conjecture were necessary) to be due to the attitude of General Buell toward Grant's order to Nelson on Sunday morning—treating it as invalid until "reiterated" by himself.

There is no room for conjecture in the matter, however, for General Buell says in his *Shiloh Reviewed*[68]: "I did not look upon him [Grant] as my commander". There is evidence also that Buell was disposed to treat the subject of Sunday's battle as something of a sham—that the resistance to the Confederate attacks was not particularly strenuous. General Tuttle of Grant's army, acted on Monday as reserve to General Buell, having under his command the two Iowa Regiments that cut their way out of the Hornets' Nest on Sunday, and one or two other regiments of Grant's army.

General Tuttle relates that "while passing over the field, April 7th", following up the advancing lines, "General Buell taunted me with not having done any fighting that amounted to anything [on Sunday]." When they came to the "clearing" in front of the Hornets' Nest and saw the ground strewn with dead, Buell "was compelled to confess

68 *The Century Magazine*, Vol. 31, p. 771.

that there must have been terrible fighting." Had General Buell passed over the ground at the Peach Orchard and over the slope in front of Sherman's first line, he would have found similar conditions to those in the "clearing" in front of the Hornets' Nest, His estimate of the vigour of the Confederate attacks on Sunday was probably based upon the feeble attack made by exhausted men which he himself saw near the Landing on Sunday night.

In Monday's battle General Buell's army constituted the left and General Grant's the right, with General Lew. Wallace's fresh division occupying the extreme right of the line—and it is worth mentioning here that at least two of Grant's regiments were sent before the battle was over to the extreme left, and one of them, under command of General Nelson, made a bayonet charge across an open field. Another of Grant's regiments, under Crittenden and near the centre, charged and captured a battery. In neither case was it necessary for General Grant to "reiterate" the requisite orders.

As to the outcome of the contest on Monday there could be no doubt, with the large accession to the ranks of the Union army—a force nearly equal to the number of men that the Confederates were able to put in line. General Grant had instructed his division commanders on Sunday night to be ready to attack early in the morning, and General Buell ordered his divisions "to move forward as soon as it was light."

Artillery fire began nearly at the same time—about five-thirty— on the extreme flanks of the Union army, though the lines were not in contact until about eight o'clock. It would not be correct to characterize the movements of the Union lines on Monday as General Beauregard characterized the movements of the Confederate lines on Sunday—the figure of the "Alpine avalanche" would not apply to the movements of either day.

However, the Union lines moved forward without serious repulses at any point, though there were some reverses on the left. The Confederates held their ground with stubbornness, occupying the line of the Purdy road until about noon. By two o'clock the battle was practically over, and an hour later the Confederates were in full retreat. Map No. 7 will give a good idea of the general movements on Monday. There was no general pursuit of the defeated army—just enough to be sure that it was a retreat in fact.

The lack of pursuit was not, however, because Grant lacked "the energy to order a pursuit", as John Codman Ropes alleges, but because Halleck's instructions did not permit pursuit; [69] hands were still "tied".

Numbers Engaged and Losses

There are two methods of estimating the strength of an army—one method excludes all non-combatants, the other includes non-combatants as essential parts of the army. On the inclusive method, the Historian and Secretary of the Shiloh National Military Park Commission[70] gives the strength of Grant's five divisions on Sunday at 39,830, and that of Johnston's army at 43,968. [71] In a note [72] in which he excludes non-combatants, the estimate is 33,000 and 40,000 respectively.

The figures last given correspond with the estimates of the two commanders—Grant in his *Memoirs*, and Johnston in his dispatch from Corinth, when about to march. In artillery, Johnston had one hundred and twenty-eight guns and Grant one hundred and twelve. Had Wallace's division come upon the field early on Sunday the two armies would have been very evenly matched, both in men and guns.

On the second day, including non-combatants and "stragglers", the figures given are: Union, 54,592; Confederate, 34,000.[73] The complete and accurate losses of the respective armies for the respective days have never been, and cannot be, stated. The losses of Grant's army by divisions, two days (except 3rd division one day) were as follows:

		Killed	Wounded	Prisoners	Total
1st division.	McClernand	285	1,372	85	1,742
2nd "	W. H. L. Wallace	270	1,173	1,306	2,749
3rd "	Lew. Wallace	41	251	4	296
4th "	Hurlbut	317	1,441	111	1,869
5th "	Sherman	325	1,277	299	1,901
6th "	Prentiss	236	928	1,008	2,172
Unassigned		39	159	17	215
Total Army Tenn.		1,513	6,601	2,830	10,944[74]
Army of the Ohio, Monday—[75]					
2nd division		88	823	7	918

69 *War of the Rebellion*: Official Records, Series 1, Vol. 10, Part 2, pp. 97, 104.
70 Reed's *The Battle of Shiloh*, p. 98.
71 Reed's *The Battle of Shiloh*, p. 110.
72 Reed's *The Battle of Shiloh*, p. 112.
73 Reed's *The Battle of Shiloh*, p. 110.
74 Reed's *The Battle of Shiloh*, p. 98.
75 Reed's *The Battle of Shiloh*, p. 102.

4th "	93	603	20	716
5th "	60	377	28	465
6th "	—	4	—	4
Total	241	1,807	55	2,103
Grand total	1,754	8,408	2,885	13,047
Army of Miss. (Confederate)	1,728	8,012	959	10,699[76]

The killed in the two days' battle are almost exactly equal; the wounded are in excess by nearly four hundred, in the Union army; and there was in the Union army an excess in prisoners, of 1,926. Eliminating the prisoners taken in the Hornets' Nest, it appears that more prisoners were taken in the open field by the Union army than by the Confederates. The loss in officers in Grant's army on Sunday from the grade of colonel up was much heavier than in the Confederate army—forty-five in the former to thirty in the latter.[77]

THE LOST DIVISION

So much has been written and said about the failure of General Wallace to get his division on the field and into the fight on the first day of the battle that the subject deserves a separate paragraph and a map of the roads over which his division marched. By reference to the map (No. 8) it will be seen that the division occupied three camps— one brigade at Crump's Landing; one at Stonylonesome, two to three miles west; and one at Adamsville, about five miles out from the Landing toward Purdy. There is no dispute about the fact that Grant on his way up the river on Sunday morning stopped at Crump's Landing to notify Wallace to be in readiness for marching orders, though Wallace makes no mention of the fact in his official report, leaving it to be inferred that he had no order from Grant in the morning. He says that from the "continuous cannonading" he "inferred a general battle"; that he was in "anticipation of an order"; and that he ordered his first and third brigades to "concentrate" on the second at Stonylonesome.[78] In his *Autobiography* General Wallace says that he was satisfied before six o'clock, from the firing "up the river", that the battle was on; and he says that at about seven o'clock, his concentration of brigades began.

The official records show that this order was not carried out, for the third brigade did not move from Adamsville until about two-thirty afternoon, when it fell in behind the first and second brigades

76 Reed's *The Battle of Shiloh*, p. 110.
77 Reed's *The Battle of Shiloh*, p. 23.
78 *War of the Rebellion*: Official Records, Series 1, Vol. 10, Part 1, p. 170.

on the march toward Snake Creek bridge, and did not join them at Stonylonesome.

About a year after the Battle of Shiloh, General Wallace had occasion to refer to the movements of his division, on that Sunday in explaining to the Department Commander the reasons for the lateness of his arrival on the field; and in his explanation he incidentally referred to Grant's call at Crump's Landing on Sunday morning, fixing the time at "about nine o'clock". [79] General Grant and the members of his staff fixed the time at seven to seven-thirty o'clock.

No special importance is to be attached to this difference in time, however, for it had no important bearing on subsequent events—it is mentioned only because it may justify a doubt as to the recollection of General Wallace in fixing the time at which he received final marching orders; namely, "11:30 a. m." It was the belief of General Grant and members of his staff that the order must have been received from a half hour to an hour earlier; though General Wallace's statement is now generally accepted. The form of order sent to Wallace can never be definitely settled, as it is nowhere a matter of record, and the original was lost in the hands of General Wallace, or through the fault of his Adjutant General.

During the year after the Battle of Shiloh, there was much criticism of General Wallace, to which he, of course, made defence. And so General Grant requested his Assistant Adjutant General, Colonel Rawlins, Colonel McPherson, Halleck's chief engineer, and Captain Rowley of his staff, each of whom had knowledge of General Wallace's movements on Sunday, to write out in detail their recollections, to be submitted to the Department Commander. Each wrote quite fully about one year after the battle, Colonel Rawlins reproducing from memory the order dictated by him as he claims, to Captain Baxter, which order was carried by the latter to Wallace. Following is the order from memory:

Major-General Wallace:

You will move forward your division from Crump's Landing, leaving a sufficient force to protect the public property at that place, to Pittsburg Landing, on the road nearest to and parallel with the river, and form in line at right angles with the river, immediately in rear of the camp of Maj. Gen. C. F. Smith's division on our right, and there await further orders. [80]

79 *War of the Rebellion*: Official Records, Series 1, Vol. 10, Part 1, p. 175.
80 *War of the Rebellion*: Official Records, Series 1, Vol. 10, Part 1, p. 185.

Captain Baxter started by boat to deliver the order "not later than nine o'clock", according to Colonel Rawlins, and reported back to Grant before "12 o'clock m."

In his official report, dated April 12, 1862, General Wallace says:

At 11:30 o'clock the anticipated order arrived, directing me to come up and take position on the right of the army and form my line of battle at a right angle with the river.[81]

Writing a year later to General Halleck, explaining the reasons for his late arrival on the field, he said: "At exactly 11:30 a. m., a quartermaster by the name of Baxter brought me an order in *writing unsigned by anybody*", the bearer of the order explaining that he received it verbally and put it in writing while on the boat.

In his *Autobiography*, General Wallace enlarges somewhat on the subject of this order, and says that it was written on paper discoloured with tobacco stains and bore the imprint of boot-heels; and he says that Baxter told him that the paper was picked up from the floor of the ladies' cabin, on the steamboat. The original order having been lost, Wallace gives the following from memory:

You will leave a sufficient force at Crump's Landing to guard the public property there: with the rest of the division inarch and form junction with the right of the army. Form line of battle at right angles with the river, and be governed by circumstances. [82]

The Rawlins form of order was reproduced from memory within one year after the event; that of Wallace, many years after—possibly forty years. Aside from the precise road mentioned and the precise position on the field designated in the Rawlins order, the two are strikingly similar—sufficiently so to suggest that the former, which had long been in print, may have been consulted to refresh the memory in preparing the latter.

Referring again to the events of Sunday as related by Colonel Rawlins, it appears that about an hour after Captain Baxter started by boat with orders to General Wallace, Grant sent a cavalry officer, familiar with the road, with a verbal message to Wallace "to hurry forward with all possible dispatch."

This officer reported back to Grant, between twelve and one o'clock, that Wallace declined to move without written orders. According to Rawlins, Captain Baxter reported back about 12 o'clock;

---

81 *War of the Rebellion*: Official Records, Series 1, Vol. 10, Part 1, p. 170.
82 Wallace's *Autobiography*, Vol. 1. p. 463.

that he delivered the orders to Wallace at about ten o'clock; that Wallace read the memorandum handed him by Captain Baxter and "appeared delighted". [83]

Immediately after the report of the cavalry officer that Wallace declined to move without written orders (Baxter's written order had not yet been delivered), Captain Rowley of Grant's staff was ordered to take the cavalry officer and two orderlies and carry instructions to Wallace, with authority to put the instructions in writing and sign them, if necessary. [84]

Captain Rowley's account of this incident is more in detail than that of Colonel Rawlins. Rowley corroborates Rawlins as to the report of the cavalry officer and says that Grant, after hearing the report, turned to him (Rowley) and said: "Captain, you will proceed to Crump's Landing and say to General Wallace that it is my orders that he bring his division up *at once*, coming up by the River road, crossing Snake Creek on the bridge". Captain Rowley says he was authorized to put the orders in writing and properly sign the same, should General Wallace require it. He was instructed to take the cavalry officer and two orderlies with him with the further instruction: "see that you do not spare horse flesh." [85] Captain Rowley gives the time of his starting on this mission at about twelve-thirty o 'clock. Colonel Rawlins fixes it at "not later than 1 o'clock p. m."

Captain Rowley's party rode directly to Wallace's headquarters at Crump's Landing, to find "no signs of a camp except one baggage wagon that was just leaving." [86] (The brigade had marched west to

---

83 *War of the Rebellion*: Official Records, Series 1, Vol. 10, Part 2, pp. 185-186.
In 1886 Captain Baxter related his recollections of this incident for publication in *The New York Mail* and *Express* (November 4, 1886) which are republished in *Battles and Leaders of the Civil War*, Vol. 1, p. 607, as follows:
"On Sunday, between the hours of 8 and 9 o'clock a. m., April 6, 1862, Adjutant General Rawlins, of General Grant's staff, requested me to go to Crump's Landing (five miles below) and order General Lew Wallace to march his command at once by the river road to Pittsburg Landing, and join the army on the right. At the same time, General Rawlins dictated the order, which was written by myself and signed by General Rawlins.
"On meeting General Wallace, I gave the order verbally, also handed to him the written order. General Wallace said he was waiting for orders, had heard the firing all the morning, and was ready to move with his command immediately—knew the road and had put it in good order."
84 *War of the Rebellion*: Official Records, Series 1, Vol. 10, Part 2, pp. 185-186.
85 *War of the Rebellion*: Official Records, Series 1, Vol. 10, Part 2, p. 179.
86 *War of the Rebellion*: Official Records, Series 1, Vol. 10, Part 2, p. 179.

Stonylonesome in the morning.) Getting directions from the driver of the wagon, the party followed the road taken by Wallace and overtook the rear of the division some five or six miles out. The division was "at a rest, sitting on each side of the road". Riding forward to the head of the column, Wallace was found "sitting upon his horse, surrounded by his staff". Although it is not so stated, it is fair to assume that the division was at rest while the cavalry was scouting to the front, as Wallace believed that he was approaching the crossing of Owl Creek, near the right of the army as it was in the morning, and where he might expect trouble.

Captain Rowley delivered his orders and stated that it had been reported to Grant that he (Wallace) had declined to march without written orders, which according to Rowley, Wallace denounced as a "damned lie!" Wallace claimed that he had taken the "*only road* he knew anything about," [87] leading in the direction of the right of the army. On learning the real situation, Wallace ordered his division to counter-march for the purpose of reaching the river road by a short-cut if possible. Captain Rowley remained with the division, acting as guide.

When Captain Rowley left the field with orders to Wallace, it was supposed that the head of the column would be found only a short distance north of Snake Creek bridge, and that Wallace would soon be in the precise position where he was expected to be, and where his presence was most needed. Two o'clock came, but no information from Wallace. Grant then sent two of the principal members of his staff, Colonel Rawlins, Assistant Adjutant General, and Colonel McPherson, Chief Engineer, to find the lost division.

These officers rode directly to Crump's Landing, not knowing whether the division had left its camp. Following directions given them there, they came upon the division counter-marching on a cross-road to the river road, at about three-thirty afternoon. Colonel Rawlins repeated to Wallace the reported refusal to march without written orders, and Wallace repeated the denial. In regard to the road taken, Wallace said, according to Rawlins, that his guide had misled him.

Soon after Rawlins and McPherson came up with the head of the column it was halted, as Rawlins states it, "for a considerable length of time, to enable it to close up and rest". There was another delay when near Snake Creek bridge "for full half an hour" while changing the

---

87 *War of the Rebellion*: Official Records, Series 1, Vol. 10, Part 1. p. 180.

position of the artillery in the column.[88]

The three officers, Rawlins, McPherson, and Rowley, agree in stating that the march of the column was very slow, and that no urging of the terms of Grants' order or the seriousness of the situation seemed to have any effect. According to Rawlins, the speed was less than "a mile and a half an hour" after he joined the column, though "the roads were in fine condition; he was marching light; his men were in buoyant spirits, ... and eager to get forward." [89]

Whatever the form of the order from General Grant to General Wallace, and however it may have been interpreted, Wallace's march began from Stonylonesome at twelve o'clock, noon, with two brigades, over the Shunpike road toward Owl Creek bridge, the third brigade falling in the rear where the road intersects from Adamsville. Captain Rowley came up to the head of the column "at rest", north of and overlooking Clear Creek valley, not Owl Creek as Wallace supposed—he was still more than three miles from Owl Creek, and the rear of the column was still at Adamsville. The counter-march began from the north side of Clear Creek, at a point marked "Smith's" (Map 8). It was necessary for the head of the column to march back about two and a half miles to find a cross-road, then about the same distance on the cross-road, before the rear could move; so it was well along in the afternoon when the last files of the third brigade left Adamsville. Colonel Rawlins and Colonel McPherson came up with Wallace on the cross-road at about three-thirty afternoon, as heretofore stated.

From a glance at the map (8) showing the roads north of Snake Creek and the relation of the roads to the battle field, it appears that the shortest possible route from Wallace's camps to the right of the army (as it was even on Sunday morning) was by the river road and Snake Creek bridge (Wallace bridge on map). Not only was the road by Owl Creek bridge much longer, but the crossing was more hazardous in case the enemy succeeded in securing the crossing and planting a battery, for the approach from the North was through a swampy valley, heavily timbered and with dense undergrowth, along a narrow road where deployment was impossible and where the column would be exposed to direct artillery fire for a distance of nearly a mile.

Had General Wallace been familiar with the roads covering the territory which it was his special province to guard, no guide could have misled him, and he would not have said that he was on "the *only*

88 *War of the Rebellion*: Official Records, Series 1, Vol. 10, Part 2, p. 187.
89 *War of the Rebellion*: Official Records, Series 1, Vol. 10, Part 2, p. 188.

road he knew anything about". His position at Crump's Landing was as much exposed to attack as was the camp at Pittsburg Landing, and he was as likely to need support as he was to be called on for support. It was of the utmost importance for the safety of his own command that he know the shortest and best road between the two camps.

Forty years after the event General Wallace was forced to confess that he had all that time been labouring under a mistake as to the position of the head of his column when the order was given to countermarch. He had all this time supposed that he was overlooking Owl Creek at the right of Sherman's lines when Captain Rowley came up and found his division "at rest", while his cavalry was scouting to the front. Instead of overlooking Owl Creek, he was overlooking the valley of Clear Creek three or four miles to the north. Of these facts General Wallace was convinced, not long before his death, by a personal inspection of the territory and the roads over which his division marched, in company with the Secretary and Historian of the Shiloh National Military Park Commission, several of his own officers, with citizens living in the locality, and with a Confederate cavalry officer who was watching his movements on that Sunday.

Strangely, General Wallace allowed this confessed error to stand in his *Autobiography*, with only partial correction.

It seems not to be generally known, though it has been a matter of official record since 1863, that General Wallace in view of General Grant's criticism of his (Wallace's) conduct at Shiloh, asked of the Secretary of War a court of inquiry. The date of the request was July 18th, 1863; but on September 16th following, the Secretary of War was asked to "suspend action in the matter",

General Wallace stating that he might be able to "satisfy General Grant upon the points involved". [90] It was on the advice of General Sherman that the request for a court of inquiry was withdrawn, and the request was never renewed, though General Grant had found no reason to modify his original criticism, down to the time of writing the chapter on Shiloh, for his *Memoirs*? [91] After the writing of that chapter, however, a letter came into General Grant's hands, written by General Lew. Wallace to General W. H. L. Wallace, dated April 5, 1862 (correct date April 4th). In this letter General Grant finds reasons for "materially" modifying the criticisms upon General Wallace, as they appear in the chapter itself, appending a footnote thereto by way of

90 *War of the Rebellion*: Official Records, Series 1, Vol. 10, Part 1, pp. 188-190.
91 *Personal Memoirs of U. S. Grant*, Vol. 1, pp. 337-338..

explanation. [92]

The writer hereof is impressed with the idea that it was the promptings of General Grant's generous nature, rather than the contents of the letter that prompted the footnote. It is not entirely clear, in view of the admissions made by General Wallace in his *Autobiography*, that the letter from General Lew. Wallace to General W. H. L. Wallace does not furnish additional ground for censure. At the moment of writing the letter the author of it must have been "simmering" in his mind the knowledge that the Confederate army was then on the march to attack Grant; and yet there was no mention in the letter of that important fact. The reader must draw his own conclusions.

---

92 *Personal Memoirs of U. 8. Grant,* Vol. 1, p. 351

MAP 1—
Showing the territory over which General Grant operated from September 4, 1861, to the time of the Battle of Shiloh, together with the Location of the Important Places Mentioned in the Text. It Also Shows the Advance of Buell's Army From Nashville to Shiloh.

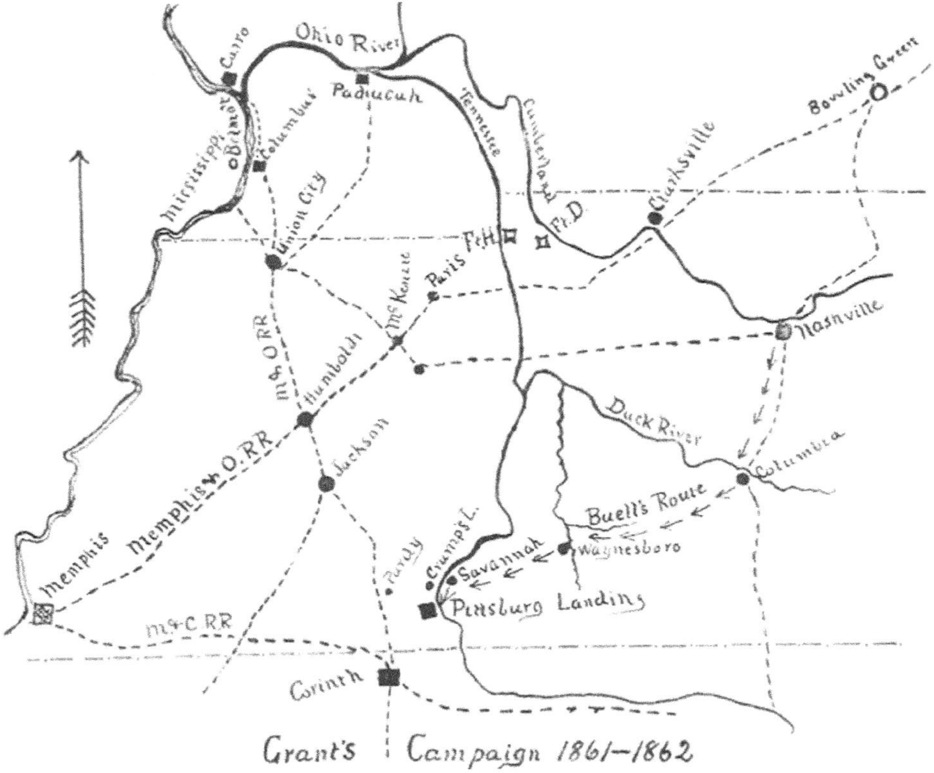

MAP 2—A VIEW OF THE PLATEAU ABOVE PITTSBURG LANDING.

SHOWING THE PRINCIPAL ROADS, CREEKS, CULTIVATED FIELDS, LOCATION OF CAMPS, WOODED CONDITION, ETC

CAMP PITTSSBURG LANDING TENN.

APRIL 6, 1862

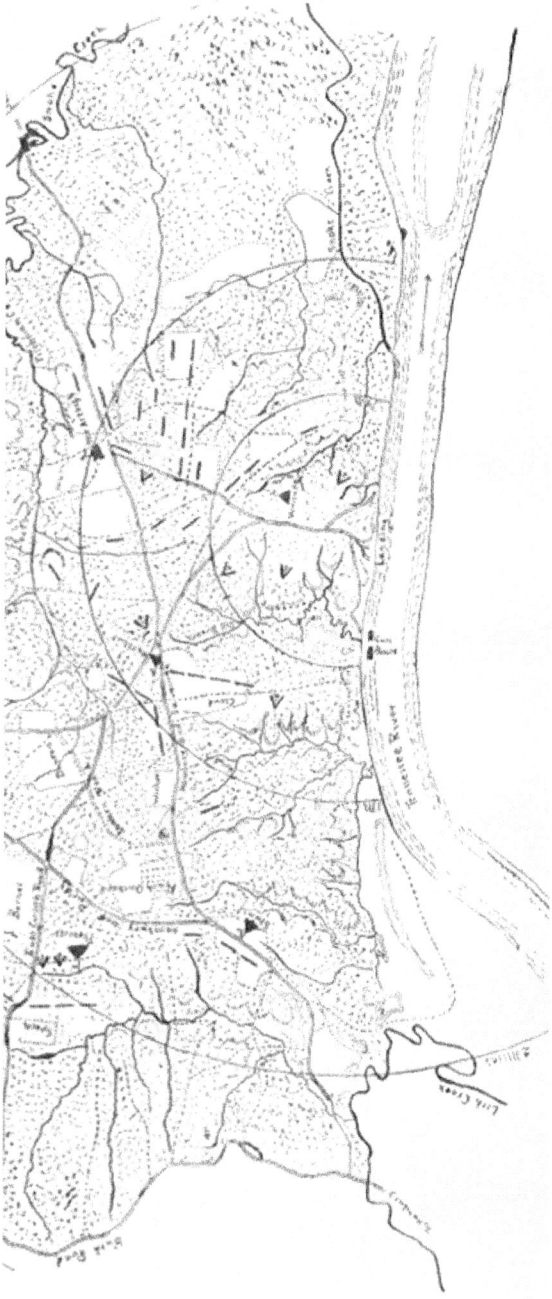

MAP 3—SHOWING THE CONFEDERATE LINES AS THEY WERE ON SATURDAY NIGHT; PRALEY FIELD WHERE THE PICKET FIGHT OCCURRED ON SUNDAY MORNING, AND THE ADVANCE TO ATTACK. ON THE UNION SIDE THE MAP SHOWS FIRST AND SECOND POSITIONS OF PRENTISS AND STUART, AND FIRST POSITIONS OF SHERMAN, MCCLERNAND, WALLACE, AND HURLBUT

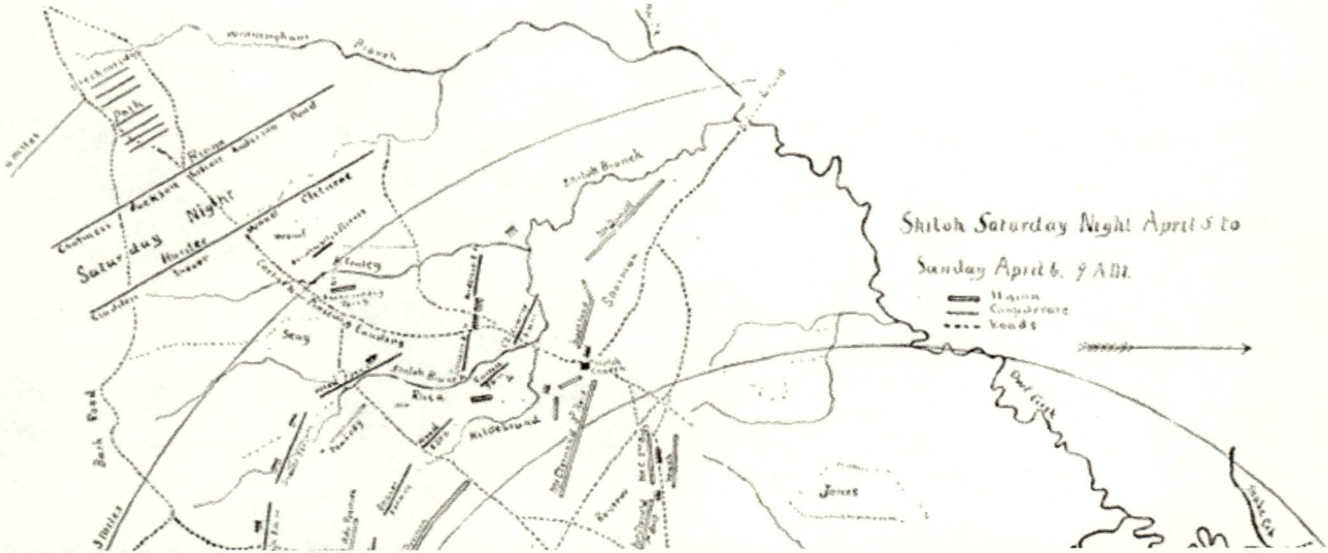

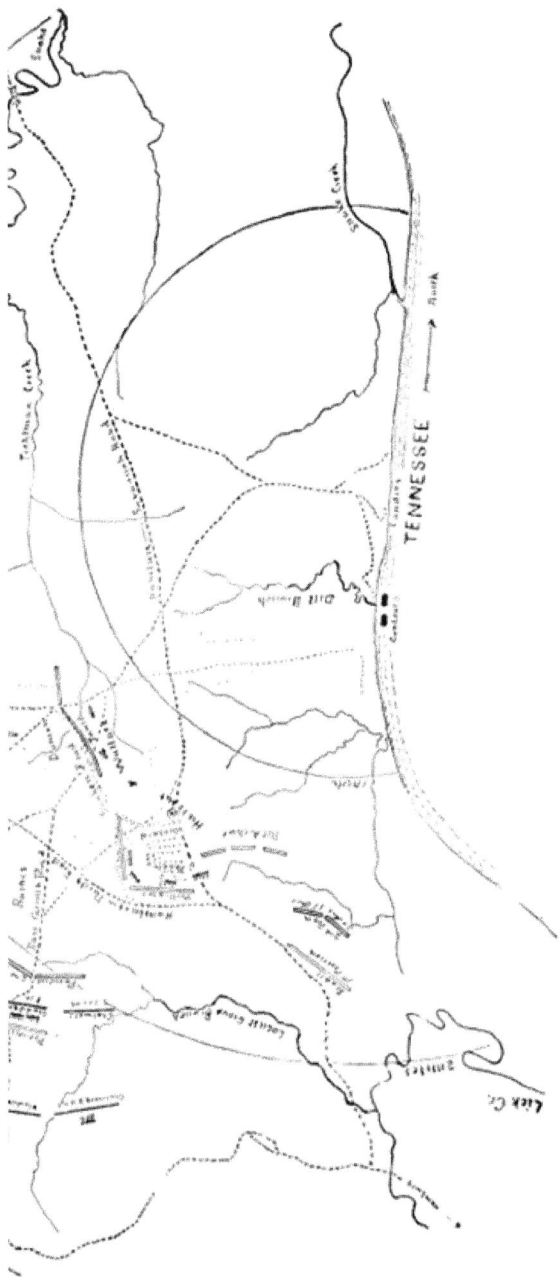

TENNESSEE

River

Shiloh Creek

Snake Creek

Tackhman Creek

Drill Branch

Locust Grove Branch

Lick Cr.

Landing

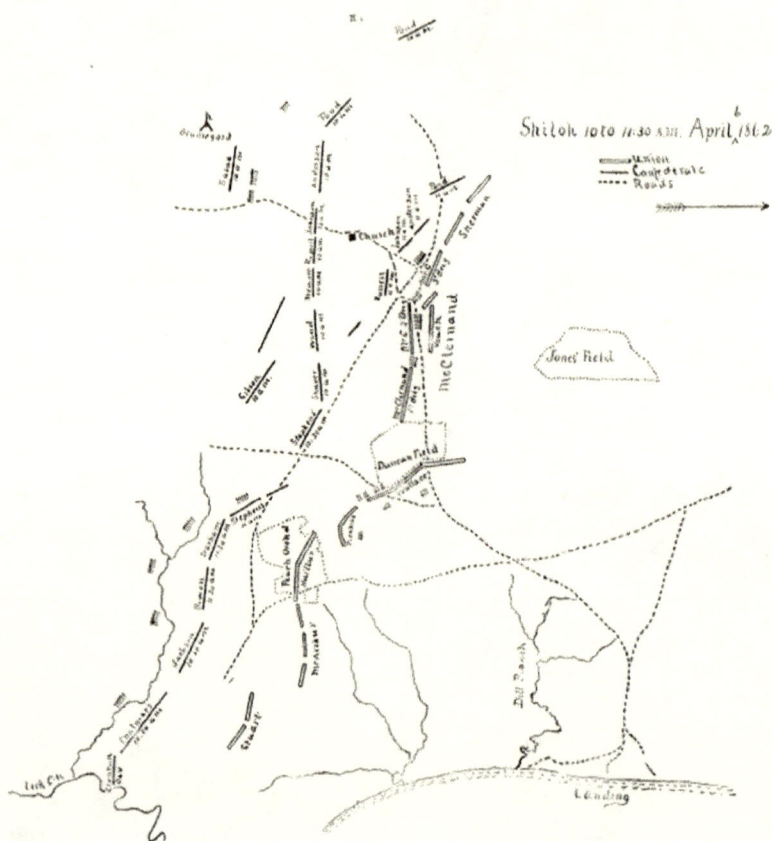

Shiloh 10 to 11.30 A.M. April 1862

MAP 4 SHOWING THE GENERAL SITUATION
UP TO ABOUT NOON ON SUNDAY

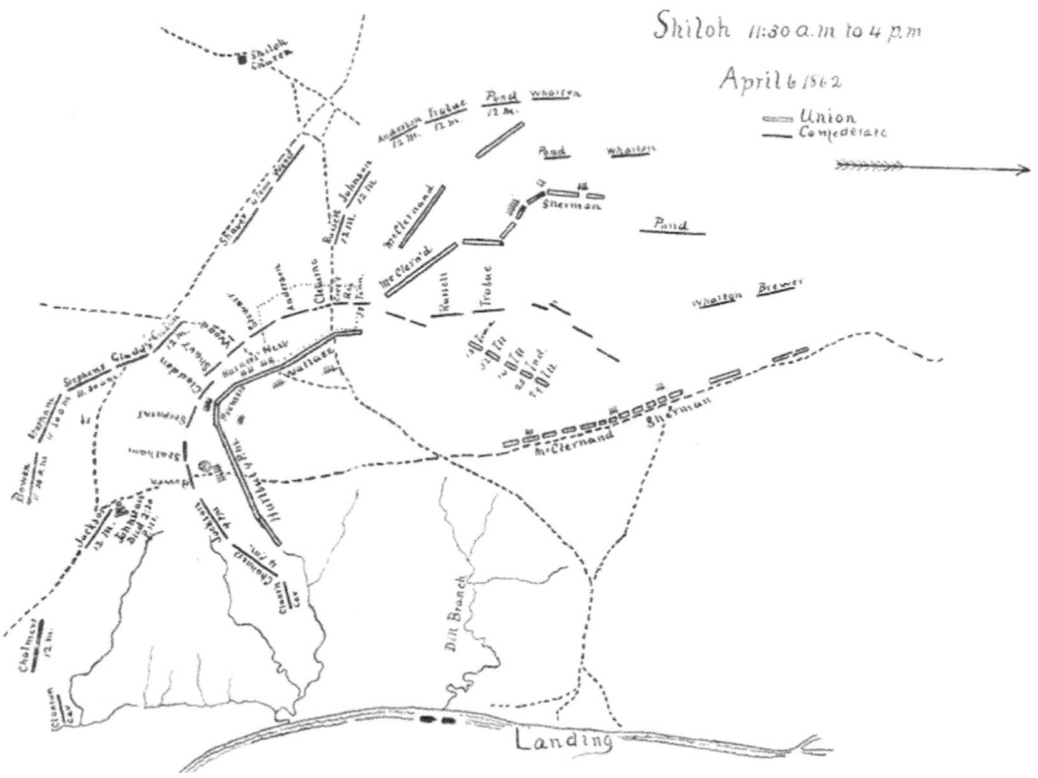

MAP 5—SHOWING CHANGE DOWN TO ABOUT FOUR O'CLOCK IN THE AFTERNOON

MAP 6—SHOWING RUGGLES'S BATTERY (62 GUNS) BOMBARDING THE HORNETS' NEST, AND THE SITUATION AT THE TIME OF THE SURRENDER AT THAT POINT. THE LINES FACING EACH OTHER ACROSS DILL BRANCH WERE THE LAST LINES OF THE DAY, SUNDAY. THE BATTERIES IN GRANT'S LINE WERE ALL THERE AS REPRESENTED: (1) MARKGRAF 6; (2) MUNCH 5; (3) POWELL 5; (4) SILFVERSPARRE 4; (5) MCALLISTER 2; (6) STONE 4; (7) DRESSER 2; (8) MANN 3; (9) SIEGE GUNS 6; (10) RICHARDSON; (11) NISPEL 2; (12) WELKER 3; (13) HICKENLOOPER 2; (14) BOUTON 4 (?). TWO OTHER BATTERIES WERE SOMEWHERE ALONG THE LINE, BUT NEVER HAVING BEEN DEFINITELY LOCATED ARE NOT REPRESENTED. (A) 36TH INDIANA SUPPORTING STONE'S BATTERY.

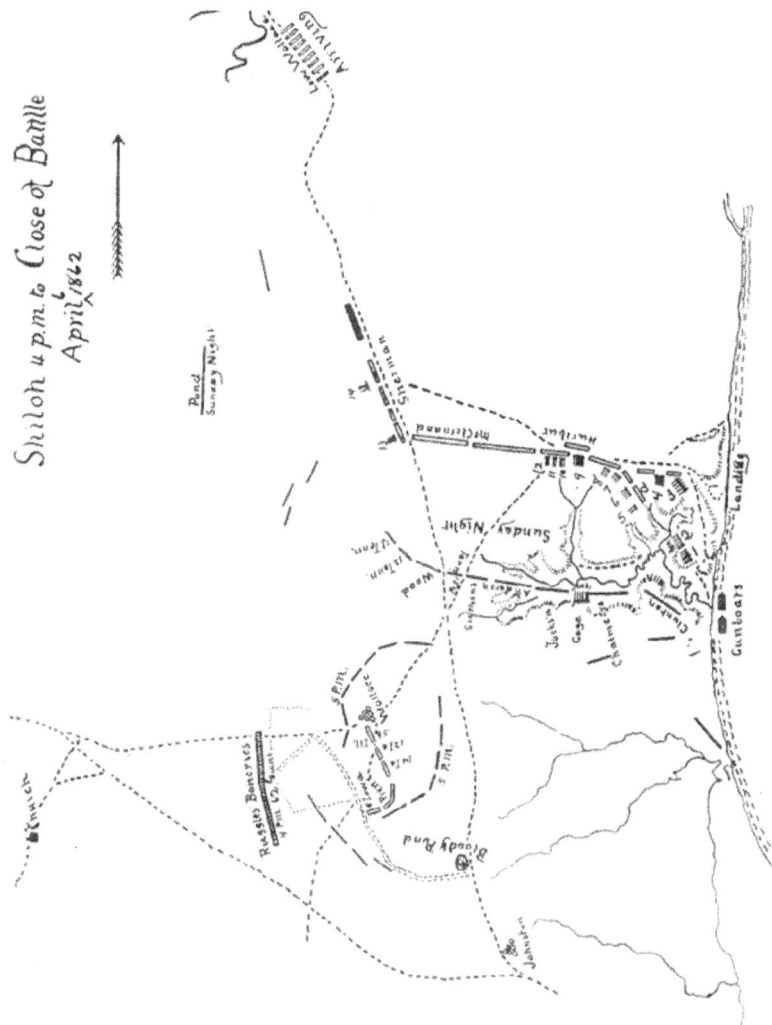

Shiloh 4 p.m. to Close of Battle
April, 1842

MAP 7—THE MOVEMENTS ON MONDAY THE 7TH ARE SO LITTLE COMPLICATED AS TO BE EASILY TRACED, WITHOUT ANALYSIS.

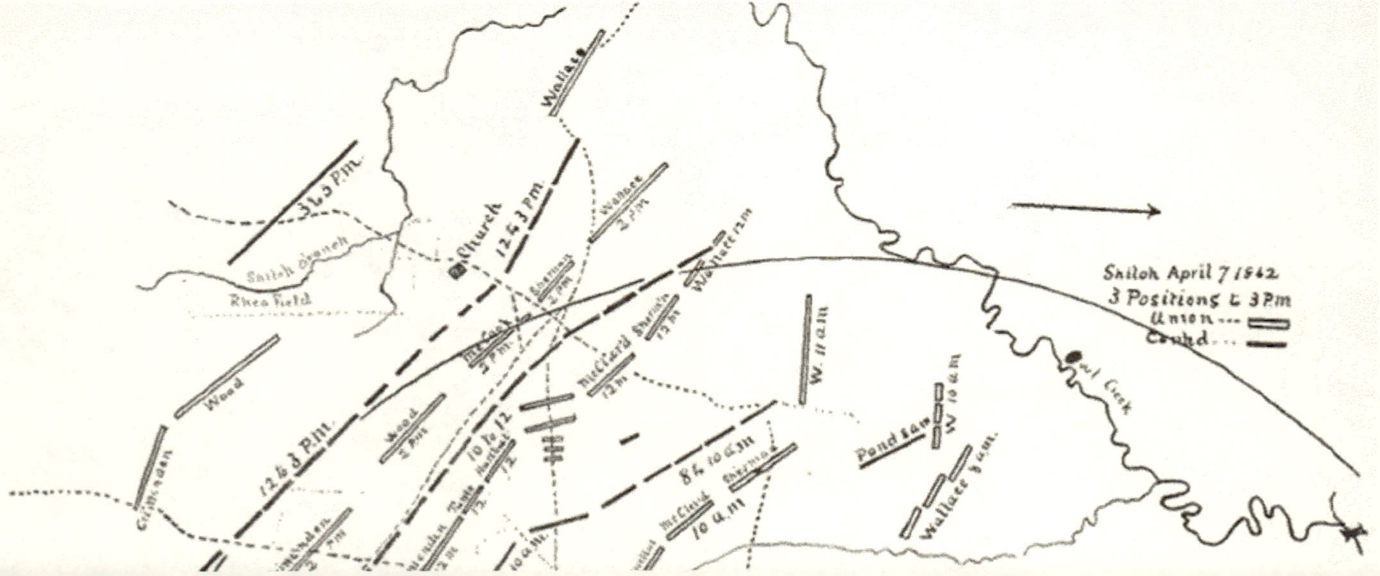

Shiloh April 7 1842
3 Positions 1 & 3 P.m
Union ---
Confd.

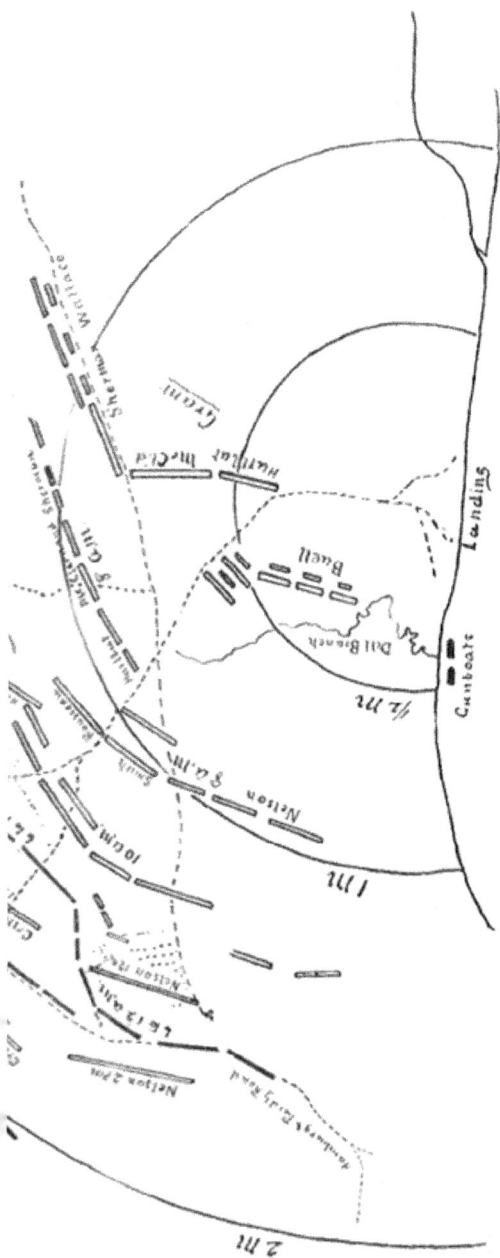

Wallace

Sherman

Crom

Hurlbut McCld

Buell

Buell

Del Branch

Landing

Gunboats

½ m

1 m

2 m

Prentiss 8 a.m.

9 a.m. Gun

South

Nelson 8 a.m.

10 a.m.

Nelson Road

L 6 12 A.M.

Nelson 2 p.m.

Hamburg-Ridge Road

MAP 8—ROADS NORTH OF OWL AND SNAKE CREEKS SHOWING LEW. WALLACE'S
ADVANCE FROM CRUMP'S LANDING, STONYLONESOME, AND ADAMSVILLE.

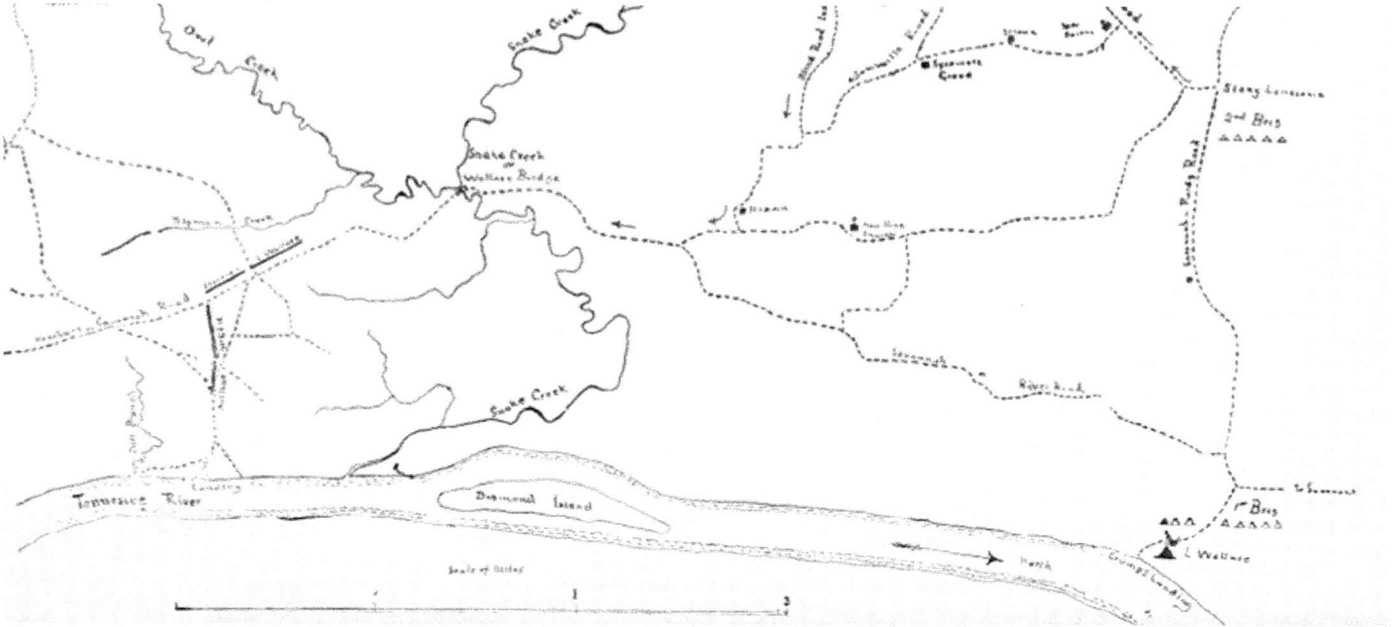

Stony Lonesome

2nd Brig

Rough Road

3rd Brig

L Wallace

North Crump's Landing

Savannah

Stony Creek

Bird's Mill

Snake Creek

Owl Creek

Snake Creek

Wallace Bridge

Snake Creek

Owl Creek

Snake Creek

Bridge

Diamond Island

Tennessee River

Pittsburg Landing

Scale of Miles

LEONAUR

ALSO FROM LEONAUR

AVAILABLE IN SOFTCOVER OR HARDCOVER WITH DUST JACKET

CAPTAIN OF THE 95th (Rifles) *by Jonathan Leach*—An officer of Wellington's Sharpshooters during the Peninsular, South of France and Waterloo Campaigns of the Napoleonic Wars.

BUGLER AND OFFICER OF THE RIFLES *by William Green & Harry Smith* With the 95th (Rifles) during the Peninsular & Waterloo Campaigns of the Napoleonic Wars

BAYONETS, BUGLES AND BONNETS by *James 'Thomas' Todd*—Experiences of hard soldiering with the 71st Foot - the Highland Light Infantry - through many battles of the Napoleonic wars including the Peninsular & Waterloo Campaigns

THE ADVENTURES OF A LIGHT DRAGOON *by George Farmer & G.R. Gleig*—A cavalryman during the Peninsular & Waterloo Campaigns, in captivity & at the siege of Bhurtpore, India

THE COMPLEAT RIFLEMAN HARRIS *by Benjamin Harris as told to & transcribed by Captain Henry Curling*—The adventures of a soldier of the 95th (Rifles) during the Peninsular Campaign of the Napoleonic Wars

WITH WELLINGTON'S LIGHT CAVALRY *by William Tomkinson*—The Experiences of an officer of the 16th Light Dragoons in the Peninsular and Waterloo campaigns of the Napoleonic Wars.

SURTEES OF THE RIFLES by *William Surtees*—A Soldier of the 95th (Rifles) in the Peninsular campaign of the Napoleonic Wars.

ENSIGN BELL IN THE PENINSULAR WAR *by George Bell*—The Experiences of a young British Soldier of the 34th Regiment 'The Cumberland Gentlemen' in the Napoleonic wars.

WITH THE LIGHT DIVISION by *John H. Cooke*—The Experiences of an Officer of the 43rd Light Infantry in the Peninsula and South of France During the Napoleonic Wars

NAPOLEON'S IMPERIAL GUARD: FROM MARENGO TO WATERLOO by *J. T. Headley*—This is the story of Napoleon's Imperial Guard from the bearskin caps of the grenadiers to the flamboyance of their mounted chasseurs, their principal characters and the men who commanded them.

BATTLES & SIEGES OF THE PENINSULAR WAR by *W. H. Fitchett*—Corunna, Busaco, Albuera, Ciudad Rodrigo, Badajos, Salamanca, San Sebastian & Others

AVAILABLE ONLINE AT **www.leonaur.com**
AND OTHER GOOD BOOK STORES

NAP-1

LEONAUR

ALSO FROM LEONAUR
AVAILABLE IN SOFTCOVER OR HARDCOVER WITH DUST JACKET

A HISTORY OF THE FRENCH & INDIAN WAR *by Arthur G. Bradley*—The Seven Years War as it was fought in the New World has always fascinated students of military history—here is the story of that confrontation.

WASHINGTON'S EARLY CAMPAIGNS *by James Hadden*—The French Post Expedition, Great Meadows and Braddock's Defeat—including Braddock's Orderly Books.

BOUQUET & THE OHIO INDIAN WAR *by Cyrus Cort & William Smith*—Two Accounts of the Campaigns of 1763-1764: Bouquet's Campaigns by Cyrus Cort & The History of Bouquet's Expeditions by William Smith.

NARRATIVES OF THE FRENCH & INDIAN WAR: 2 *by David Holden, Samuel Jenks, Lemuel Lyon, Mary Cochrane Rogers & Henry T. Blake*—Contains The Diary of Sergeant David Holden, Captain Samuel Jenks' Journal, The Journal of Lemuel Lyon, Journal of a French Officer at the Siege of Quebec, A Battle Fought on Snowshoes & The Battle of Lake George.

NARRATIVES OF THE FRENCH & INDIAN WAR *by Brown, Eastburn, Hawks & Putnam*—Ranger Brown's Narrative, The Adventures of Robert Eastburn, The Journal of Rufus Putnam—Provincial Infantry & Orderly Book and Journal of Major John Hawks on the Ticonderoga-Crown Point Campaign.

THE 7TH (QUEEN'S OWN) HUSSARS: Volume 1—1688-1792 *by C. R. B. Barrett*—As Dragoons During the Flanders Campaign, War of the Austrian Succession and the Seven Years War.

INDIA'S FREE LANCES *by H. G. Keene*—European Mercenary Commanders in Hindustan 1770-1820.

THE BENGAL EUROPEAN REGIMENT *by P. R. Innes*—An Elite Regiment of the Honourable East India Company 1756-1858.

MUSKET & TOMAHAWK *by Francis Parkman*—A Military History of the French & Indian War, 1753-1760.

THE BLACK WATCH AT TICONDEROGA *by Frederick B. Richards*—Campaigns in the French & Indian War.

QUEEN'S RANGERS *by Frederick B. Richards*—John Simcoe and his Rangers During the Revolutionary War for America.

AVAILABLE ONLINE AT **www.leonaur.com**
AND FROM ALL GOOD BOOK STORES   07/09

LEONAUR

ALSO FROM LEONAUR
AVAILABLE IN SOFTCOVER OR HARDCOVER WITH DUST JACKET

JOURNALS OF ROBERT ROGERS OF THE RANGERS *by Robert Rogers*—The exploits of Rogers & the Rangers in his own words during 1755-1761 in the French & Indian War.

GALLOPING GUNS *by James Young*—The Experiences of an Officer of the Bengal Horse Artillery During the Second Maratha War 1804-1805.

GORDON *by Demetrius Charles Boulger*—The Career of Gordon of Khartoum.

THE BATTLE OF NEW ORLEANS *by Zachary F. Smith*—The final major engagement of the War of 1812.

THE TWO WARS OF MRS DUBERLY *by Frances Isabella Duberly*—An Intrepid Victorian Lady's Experience of the Crimea and Indian Mutiny.

WITH THE GUARDS' BRIGADE DURING THE BOER WAR *by Edward P. Lowry*—On Campaign from Bloemfontein to Koomati Poort and Back.

THE REBELLIOUS DUCHESS *by Paul F. S. Dermoncourt*—The Adventures of the Duchess of Berri and Her Attempt to Overthrow French Monarchy.

MEN OF THE MUTINY *by John Tulloch Nash & Henry Metcalfe*—Two Accounts of the Great Indian Mutiny of 1857: Fighting with the Bengal Yeomanry Cavalry & Private Metcalfe at Lucknow.

CAMPAIGN IN THE CRIMEA *by George Shuldham Peard*—The Recollections of an Officer of the 20th Regiment of Foot.

WITHIN SEBASTOPOL *by K. Hodasevich*—A Narrative of the Campaign in the Crimea, and of the Events of the Siege.

WITH THE CAVALRY TO AFGHANISTAN *by William Taylor*—The Experiences of a Trooper of H. M. 4th Light Dragoons During the First Afghan War.

THE CAWNPORE MAN *by Mowbray Thompson*—A First Hand Account of the Siege and Massacre During the Indian Mutiny By One of Four Survivors.

BRIGADE COMMANDER: AFGHANISTAN *by Henry Brooke*—The Journal of the Commander of the 2nd Infantry Brigade, Kandahar Field Force During the Second Afghan War.

BANCROFT OF THE BENGAL HORSE ARTILLERY *by N. W. Bancroft*—An Account of the First Sikh War 1845-1846.

AVAILABLE ONLINE AT www.leonaur.com
AND FROM ALL GOOD BOOK STORES

07/09

LEONAUR

ALSO FROM LEONAUR
AVAILABLE IN SOFTCOVER OR HARDCOVER WITH DUST JACKET

AFGHANISTAN: THE BELEAGUERED BRIGADE *by G. R. Gleig*—An Account of Sale's Brigade During the First Afghan War.

IN THE RANKS OF THE C. I. V *by Erskine Childers*—With the City Imperial Volunteer Battery (Honourable Artillery Company) in the Second Boer War.

THE BENGAL NATIVE ARMY *by F. G. Cardew*—An Invaluable Reference Resource.

THE 7TH (QUEEN'S OWN) HUSSARS: Volume 4—1688-1914 *by C. R. B. Barrett*—Uniforms, Equipment, Weapons, Traditions, the Services of Notable Officers and Men & the Appendices to All Volumes—Volume 4: 1688-1914.

THE SWORD OF THE CROWN *by Eric W. Sheppard*—A History of the British Army to 1914.

THE 7TH (QUEEN'S OWN) HUSSARS: Volume 3—1818-1914 *by C. R. B. Barrett*—On Campaign During the Canadian Rebellion, the Indian Mutiny, the Sudan, Matabeleland, Mashonaland and the Boer War Volume 3: 1818-1914.

THE KHARTOUM CAMPAIGN *by Bennet Burleigh*—A Special Correspondent's View of the Reconquest of the Sudan by British and Egyptian Forces under Kitchener—1898.

EL PUCHERO *by Richard McSherry*—The Letters of a Surgeon of Volunteers During Scott's Campaign of the American-Mexican War 1847-1848.

RIFLEMAN SAHIB *by E. Maude*—The Recollections of an Officer of the Bombay Rifles During the Southern Mahratta Campaign, Second Sikh War, Persian Campaign and Indian Mutiny.

THE KING'S HUSSAR *by Edwin Mole*—The Recollections of a 14th (King's) Hussar During the Victorian Era.

JOHN COMPANY'S CAVALRYMAN *by William Johnson*—The Experiences of a British Soldier in the Crimea, the Persian Campaign and the Indian Mutiny.

COLENSO & DURNFORD'S ZULU WAR *by Frances E. Colenso & Edward Durnford*—The first and possibly the most important history of the Zulu War.

U. S. DRAGOON *by Samuel E. Chamberlain*—Experiences in the Mexican War 1846-48 and on the South Western Frontier.

AVAILABLE ONLINE AT **www.leonaur.com**
AND FROM ALL GOOD BOOK STORES
07/09

LEONAUR

ALSO FROM LEONAUR
AVAILABLE IN SOFTCOVER OR HARDCOVER WITH DUST JACKET

THE 2ND MAORI WAR: 1860-1861 *by Robert Carey*—The Second Maori War, or First Taranaki War, one more bloody instalment of the conflicts between European settlers and the indigenous Maori people.

A JOURNAL OF THE SECOND SIKH WAR *by Daniel A. Sandford*—The Experiences of an Ensign of the 2nd Bengal European Regiment During the Campaign in the Punjab, India, 1848-49.

THE LIGHT INFANTRY OFFICER *by John H. Cooke*—The Experiences of an Officer of the 43rd Light Infantry in America During the War of 1812.

BUSHVELDT CARBINEERS *by George Witton*—The War Against the Boers in South Africa and the 'Breaker' Morant Incident.

LAKE'S CAMPAIGNS IN INDIA *by Hugh Pearse*—The Second Anglo Maratha War, 1803-1807.

BRITAIN IN AFGHANISTAN 1: THE FIRST AFGHAN WAR 1839-42 *by Archibald Forbes*—From invasion to destruction-a British military disaster.

BRITAIN IN AFGHANISTAN 2: THE SECOND AFGHAN WAR 1878-80 *by Archibald Forbes*—This is the history of the Second Afghan War-another episode of British military history typified by savagery, massacre, siege and battles.

UP AMONG THE PANDIES *by Vivian Dering Majendie*—Experiences of a British Officer on Campaign During the Indian Mutiny, 1857-1858.

MUTINY: 1857 *by James Humphries*—Authentic Voices from the Indian Mutiny-First Hand Accounts of Battles, Sieges and Personal Hardships.

BLOW THE BUGLE, DRAW THE SWORD *by W. H. G. Kingston*—The Wars, Campaigns, Regiments and Soldiers of the British & Indian Armies During the Victorian Era, 1839-1898.

WAR BEYOND THE DRAGON PAGODA *by Major J. J. Snodgrass*—A Personal Narrative of the First Anglo-Burmese War 1824 - 1826.

THE HERO OF ALIWAL *by James Humphries*—The Campaigns of Sir Harry Smith in India, 1843-1846, During the Gwalior War & the First Sikh War.

ALL FOR A SHILLING A DAY *by Donald F. Featherstone*—The story of H.M. 16th, the Queen's Lancers During the first Sikh War 1845-1846.

AVAILABLE ONLINE AT www.leonaur.com
AND FROM ALL GOOD BOOK STORES
07/09

LEONAUR

ALSO FROM LEONAUR
AVAILABLE IN SOFTCOVER OR HARDCOVER WITH DUST JACKET

THE FALL OF THE MOGHUL EMPIRE OF HINDUSTAN *by H. G. Keene*—By the beginning of the nineteenth century, as British and Indian armies under Lake and Wellesley dominated the scene, a little over half a century of conflict brought the Moghul Empire to its knees.

LADY SALE'S AFGHANISTAN *by Florentia Sale*—An Indomitable Victorian Lady's Account of the Retreat from Kabul During the First Afghan War.

THE CAMPAIGN OF MAGENTA AND SOLFERINO 1859 *by Harold Carmichael Wylly*—The Decisive Conflict for the Unification of Italy.

FRENCH'S CAVALRY CAMPAIGN *by J. G. Maydon*—A Special Correspondent's View of British Army Mounted Troops During the Boer War.

CAVALRY AT WATERLOO *by Sir Evelyn Wood*—British Mounted Troops During the Campaign of 1815.

THE SUBALTERN *by George Robert Gleig*—The Experiences of an Officer of the 85th Light Infantry During the Peninsular War.

NAPOLEON AT BAY, 1814 *by F. Loraine Petre*—The Campaigns to the Fall of the First Empire.

NAPOLEON AND THE CAMPAIGN OF 1806 *by Colonel Vachée*—The Napoleonic Method of Organisation and Command to the Battles of Jena & Auerstädt.

THE COMPLETE ADVENTURES IN THE CONNAUGHT RANGERS *by William Grattan*—The 88th Regiment during the Napoleonic Wars by a Serving Officer.

BUGLER AND OFFICER OF THE RIFLES *by William Green & Harry Smith*—With the 95th (Rifles) during the Peninsular & Waterloo Campaigns of the Napoleonic Wars.

NAPOLEONIC WAR STORIES *by Sir Arthur Quiller-Couch*—Tales of soldiers, spies, battles & sieges from the Peninsular & Waterloo campaigns.

CAPTAIN OF THE 95TH (RIFLES) *by Jonathan Leach*—An officer of Wellington's sharpshooters during the Peninsular, South of France and Waterloo campaigns of the Napoleonic wars.

RIFLEMAN COSTELLO *by Edward Costello*—The adventures of a soldier of the 95th (Rifles) in the Peninsular & Waterloo Campaigns of the Napoleonic wars.

AVAILABLE ONLINE AT **www.leonaur.com**
AND FROM ALL GOOD BOOK STORES
07/09

LEONAUR

ALSO FROM LEONAUR
AVAILABLE IN SOFTCOVER OR HARDCOVER WITH DUST JACKET

AT THEM WITH THE BAYONET *by Donald F. Featherstone*—The first Anglo-Sikh War 1845-1846.

STEPHEN CRANE'S BATTLES *by Stephen Crane*—Nine Decisive Battles Recounted by the Author of 'The Red Badge of Courage'.

THE GURKHA WAR *by H. T. Prinsep*—The Anglo-Nepalese Conflict in North East India 1814-1816.

FIRE & BLOOD *by G. R. Gleig*—The burning of Washington & the battle of New Orleans, 1814, through the eyes of a young British soldier.

SOUND ADVANCE! *by Joseph Anderson*—Experiences of an officer of HM 50th regiment in Australia, Burma & the Gwalior war.

THE CAMPAIGN OF THE INDUS *by Thomas Holdsworth*—Experiences of a British Officer of the 2nd (Queen's Royal) Regiment in the Campaign to Place Shah Shuja on the Throne of Afghanistan 1838 - 1840.

WITH THE MADRAS EUROPEAN REGIMENT IN BURMA *by John Butler*—The Experiences of an Officer of the Honourable East India Company's Army During the First Anglo-Burmese War 1824 - 1826.

IN ZULULAND WITH THE BRITISH ARMY *by Charles L. Norris-Newman*—The Anglo-Zulu war of 1879 through the first-hand experiences of a special correspondent.

BESIEGED IN LUCKNOW *by Martin Richard Gubbins*—The first Anglo-Sikh War 1845-1846.

A TIGER ON HORSEBACK *by L. March Phillips*—The Experiences of a Trooper & Officer of Rimington's Guides - The Tigers - during the Anglo-Boer war 1899 - 1902.

SEPOYS, SIEGE & STORM *by Charles John Griffiths*—The Experiences of a young officer of H.M.'s 61st Regiment at Ferozepore, Delhi ridge and at the fall of Delhi during the Indian mutiny 1857.

CAMPAIGNING IN ZULULAND *by W. E. Montague*—Experiences on campaign during the Zulu war of 1879 with the 94th Regiment.

THE STORY OF THE GUIDES *by G.J. Younghusband*—The Exploits of the Soldiers of the famous Indian Army Regiment from the northwest frontier 1847 - 1900.

AVAILABLE ONLINE AT **www.leonaur.com**
AND FROM ALL GOOD BOOK STORES

07/09

LEONAUR

ALSO FROM LEONAUR
AVAILABLE IN SOFTCOVER OR HARDCOVER WITH DUST JACKET

ZULU:1879 *by D.C.F. Moodie & the Leonaur Editors*—The Anglo-Zulu War of 1879 from contemporary sources: First Hand Accounts, Interviews, Dispatches, Official Documents & Newspaper Reports.

THE RED DRAGOON *by W.J. Adams*—With the 7th Dragoon Guards in the Cape of Good Hope against the Boers & the Kaffir tribes during the 'war of the axe' 1843-48'.

THE RECOLLECTIONS OF SKINNER OF SKINNER'S HORSE *by James Skinner*—James Skinner and his 'Yellow Boys' Irregular cavalry in the wars of India between the British, Mahratta, Rajput, Mogul, Sikh & Pindarree Forces.

A CAVALRY OFFICER DURING THE SEPOY REVOLT *by A. R. D. Mackenzie*—Experiences with the 3rd Bengal Light Cavalry, the Guides and Sikh Irregular Cavalry from the outbreak to Delhi and Lucknow.

A NORFOLK SOLDIER IN THE FIRST SIKH WAR *by J W Baldwin*—Experiences of a private of H.M. 9th Regiment of Foot in the battles for the Punjab, India 1845-6.

TOMMY ATKINS' WAR STORIES: 14 FIRST HAND ACCOUNTS—Fourteen first hand accounts from the ranks of the British Army during Queen Victoria's Empire.

THE WATERLOO LETTERS *by H. T. Siborne*—Accounts of the Battle by British Officers for its Foremost Historian.

NEY: GENERAL OF CAVALRY VOLUME 1—1769-1799 *by Antoine Bulos*—The Early Career of a Marshal of the First Empire.

NEY: MARSHAL OF FRANCE VOLUME 2—1799-1805 *by Antoine Bulos*—The Early Career of a Marshal of the First Empire.

AIDE-DE-CAMP TO NAPOLEON *by Philippe-Paul de Ségur*—For anyone interested in the Napoleonic Wars this book, written by one who was intimate with the strategies and machinations of the Emperor, will be essential reading.

TWILIGHT OF EMPIRE *by Sir Thomas Ussher & Sir George Cockburn*—Two accounts of Napoleon's Journeys in Exile to Elba and St. Helena: Narrative of Events by Sir Thomas Ussher & Napoleon's Last Voyage: Extract of a diary by Sir George Cockburn.

PRIVATE WHEELER *by William Wheeler*—The letters of a soldier of the 51st Light Infantry during the Peninsular War & at Waterloo.

AVAILABLE ONLINE AT www.leonaur.com
AND FROM ALL GOOD BOOK STORES

07/09

ALSO FROM LEONAUR
AVAILABLE IN SOFTCOVER OR HARDCOVER WITH DUST JACKET

OFFICERS & GENTLEMEN *by Peter Hawker & William Graham*—Two Accounts of British Officers During the Peninsula War: Officer of Light Dragoons by Peter Hawker & Campaign in Portugal and Spain by William Graham .

THE WALCHEREN EXPEDITION *by Anonymous*—The Experiences of a British Officer of the 81st Regt. During the Campaign in the Low Countries of 1809.

LADIES OF WATERLOO *by Charlotte A. Eaton, Magdalene de Lancey & Juana Smith*—The Experiences of Three Women During the Campaign of 1815: Waterloo Days by Charlotte A. Eaton, A Week at Waterloo by Magdalene de Lancey & Juana's Story by Juana Smith.

JOURNAL OF AN OFFICER IN THE KING'S GERMAN LEGION *by John Frederick Hering*—Recollections of Campaigning During the Napoleonic Wars.

JOURNAL OF AN ARMY SURGEON IN THE PENINSULAR WAR *by Charles Boutflower*—The Recollections of a British Army Medical Man on Campaign During the Napoleonic Wars.

ON CAMPAIGN WITH MOORE AND WELLINGTON *by Anthony Hamilton*—The Experiences of a Soldier of the 43rd Regiment During the Peninsular War.

THE ROAD TO AUSTERLITZ *by R. G. Burton*—Napoleon's Campaign of 1805.

SOLDIERS OF NAPOLEON *by A. J. Doisy De Villargennes & Arthur Chuquet*—The Experiences of the Men of the French First Empire: Under the Eagles by A. J. Doisy De Villargennes & Voices of 1812 by Arthur Chuquet .

INVASION OF FRANCE, 1814 *by F. W. O. Maycock*—The Final Battles of the Napoleonic First Empire.

LEIPZIG—A CONFLICT OF TITANS *by Frederic Shoberl*—A Personal Experience of the 'Battle of the Nations' During the Napoleonic Wars, October 14th-19th, 1813.

SLASHERS *by Charles Cadell*—The Campaigns of the 28th Regiment of Foot During the Napoleonic Wars by a Serving Officer.

BATTLE IMPERIAL *by Charles William Vane*—The Campaigns in Germany & France for the Defeat of Napoleon 1813-1814.

SWIFT & BOLD *by Gibbes Rigaud*—The 60th Rifles During the Peninsula War.

AVAILABLE ONLINE AT www.leonaur.com
AND FROM ALL GOOD BOOK STORES

07/09

LEONAUR

ALSO FROM LEONAUR
AVAILABLE IN SOFTCOVER OR HARDCOVER WITH DUST JACKET

ADVENTURES OF A YOUNG RIFLEMAN *by Johann Christian Maempel*—The Experiences of a Saxon in the French & British Armies During the Napoleonic Wars.

THE HUSSAR *by Norbert Landsheit & G. R. Gleig*—A German Cavalryman in British Service Throughout the Napoleonic Wars.

RECOLLECTIONS OF THE PENINSULA *by Moyle Sherer*—An Officer of the 34th Regiment of Foot—'The Cumberland Gentlemen'—on Campaign Against Napoleon's French Army in Spain.

MARINE OF REVOLUTION & CONSULATE *by Moreau de Jonnès*—The Recollections of a French Soldier of the Revolutionary Wars 1791-1804.

GENTLEMEN IN RED *by John Dobbs & Robert Knowles*—Two Accounts of British Infantry Officers During the Peninsular War Recollections of an Old 52nd Man by John Dobbs An Officer of Fusiliers by Robert Knowles.

CORPORAL BROWN'S CAMPAIGNS IN THE LOW COUNTRIES *by Robert Brown*—Recollections of a Coldstream Guard in the Early Campaigns Against Revolutionary France 1793-1795.

THE 7TH (QUEENS OWN) HUSSARS: Volume 2—1793-1815 *by C. R. B. Barrett*—During the Campaigns in the Low Countries & the Peninsula and Waterloo Campaigns of the Napoleonic Wars. Volume 2: 1793-1815.

THE MARENGO CAMPAIGN 1800 *by Herbert H. Sargent*—The Victory that Completed the Austrian Defeat in Italy.

DONALDSON OF THE 94TH—SCOTS BRIGADE *by Joseph Donaldson*—The Recollections of a Soldier During the Peninsula & South of France Campaigns of the Napoleonic Wars.

A CONSCRIPT FOR EMPIRE *by Philippe as told to Johann Christian Maempel*—The Experiences of a Young German Conscript During the Napoleonic Wars.

JOURNAL OF THE CAMPAIGN OF 1815 *by Alexander Cavalié Mercer*—The Experiences of an Officer of the Royal Horse Artillery During the Waterloo Campaign.

NAPOLEON'S CAMPAIGNS IN POLAND 1806-7 *by Robert Wilson*—The campaign in Poland from the Russian side of the conflict.

AVAILABLE ONLINE AT **www.leonaur.com**
AND FROM ALL GOOD BOOK STORES
07/09

LEONAUR

ALSO FROM LEONAUR
AVAILABLE IN SOFTCOVER OR HARDCOVER WITH DUST JACKET

OMPTEDA OF THE KING'S GERMAN LEGION *by Christian von Ompteda*—A Hanoverian Officer on Campaign Against Napoleon.

LIEUTENANT SIMMONS OF THE 95TH (RIFLES) *by George Simmons*—Recollections of the Peninsula, South of France & Waterloo Campaigns of the Napoleonic Wars.

A HORSEMAN FOR THE EMPEROR *by Jean Baptiste Gazzola*—A Cavalryman of Napoleon's Army on Campaign Throughout the Napoleonic Wars.

SERGEANT LAWRENCE *by William Lawrence*—With the 40th Regt. of Foot in South America, the Peninsular War & at Waterloo.

CAMPAIGNS WITH THE FIELD TRAIN *by Richard D. Henegan*—Experiences of a British Officer During the Peninsula and Waterloo Campaigns of the Napoleonic Wars.

CAVALRY SURGEON *by S. D. Broughton*—On Campaign Against Napoleon in the Peninsula & South of France During the Napoleonic Wars 1812-1814.

MEN OF THE RIFLES *by Thomas Knight, Henry Curling & Jonathan Leach*—The Reminiscences of Thomas Knight of the 95th (Rifles) by Thomas Knight, Henry Curling's Anecdotes by Henry Curling & The Field Services of the Rifle Brigade from its Formation to Waterloo by Jonathan Leach.

THE ULM CAMPAIGN 1805 *by F. N. Maude*—Napoleon and the Defeat of the Austrian Army During the 'War of the Third Coalition'.

SOLDIERING WITH THE 'DIVISION' *by Thomas Garrety*—The Military Experiences of an Infantryman of the 43rd Regiment During the Napoleonic Wars.

SERGEANT MORRIS OF THE 73RD FOOT *by Thomas Morris*—The Experiences of a British Infantryman During the Napoleonic Wars-Including Campaigns in Germany and at Waterloo.

A VOICE FROM WATERLOO *by Edward Cotton*—The Personal Experiences of a British Cavalryman Who Became a Battlefield Guide and Authority on the Campaign of 1815.

NAPOLEON AND HIS MARSHALS *by J. T. Headley*—The Men of the First Empire.

AVAILABLE ONLINE AT www.leonaur.com
AND FROM ALL GOOD BOOK STORES
07/09

LEONAUR

ALSO FROM LEONAUR
AVAILABLE IN SOFTCOVER OR HARDCOVER WITH DUST JACKET

COLBORNE: A SINGULAR TALENT FOR WAR *by John Colborne*—The Napoleonic Wars Career of One of Wellington's Most Highly Valued Officers in Egypt, Holland, Italy, the Peninsula and at Waterloo.

NAPOLEON'S RUSSIAN CAMPAIGN *by Philippe Henri de Segur*—The Invasion, Battles and Retreat by an Aide-de-Camp on the Emperor's Staff.

WITH THE LIGHT DIVISION *by John H. Cooke*—The Experiences of an Officer of the 43rd Light Infantry in the Peninsula and South of France During the Napoleonic Wars.

WELLINGTON AND THE PYRENEES CAMPAIGN VOLUME I: FROM VITORIA TO THE BIDASSOA *by F. C. Beatson*—The final phase of the campaign in the Iberian Peninsula.

WELLINGTON AND THE INVASION OF FRANCE VOLUME II: THE BIDASSOA TO THE BATTLE OF THE NIVELLE *by F. C. Beatson*—The final phase of the campaign in the Iberian Peninsula.

WELLINGTON AND THE FALL OF FRANCE VOLUME III: THE GAVES AND THE BATTLE OF ORTHEZ *by F. C. Beatson*—The final phase of the campaign in the Iberian Peninsula.

NAPOLEON'S IMPERIAL GUARD: FROM MARENGO TO WATERLOO *by J. T. Headley*—The story of Napoleon's Imperial Guard and the men who commanded them.

BATTLES & SIEGES OF THE PENINSULAR WAR *by W. H. Fitchett*—Corunna, Busaco, Albuera, Ciudad Rodrigo, Badajos, Salamanca, San Sebastian & Others.

SERGEANT GUILLEMARD: THE MAN WHO SHOT NELSON? *by Robert Guillemard*—A Soldier of the Infantry of the French Army of Napoleon on Campaign Throughout Europe.

WITH THE GUARDS ACROSS THE PYRENEES *by Robert Batty*—The Experiences of a British Officer of Wellington's Army During the Battles for the Fall of Napoleonic France, 1813 .

A STAFF OFFICER IN THE PENINSULA *by E. W. Buckham*—An Officer of the British Staff Corps Cavalry During the Peninsula Campaign of the Napoleonic Wars.

THE LEIPZIG CAMPAIGN: 1813—NAPOLEON AND THE "BATTLE OF THE NATIONS" *by F. N. Maude*—Colonel Maude's analysis of Napoleon's campaign of 1813 around Leipzig.

AVAILABLE ONLINE AT www.leonaur.com
AND FROM ALL GOOD BOOK STORES
07/09

LEONAUR

ALSO FROM LEONAUR
AVAILABLE IN SOFTCOVER OR HARDCOVER WITH DUST JACKET

BUGEAUD: A PACK WITH A BATON *by Thomas Robert Bugeaud*—The Early Campaigns of a Soldier of Napoleon's Army Who Would Become a Marshal of France.

WATERLOO RECOLLECTIONS *by Frederick Llewellyn*—Rare First Hand Accounts, Letters, Reports and Retellings from the Campaign of 1815.

SERGEANT NICOL *by Daniel Nicol*—The Experiences of a Gordon Highlander During the Napoleonic Wars in Egypt, the Peninsula and France.

THE JENA CAMPAIGN: 1806 *by F. N. Maude*—The Twin Battles of Jena & Auerstadt Between Napoleon's French and the Prussian Army.

PRIVATE O'NEIL *by Charles O'Neil*—The recollections of an Irish Rogue of H. M. 28th Regt.—The Slashers—during the Peninsula & Waterloo campaigns of the Napoleonic war.

ROYAL HIGHLANDER *by James Anton*—A soldier of H.M 42nd (Royal) Highlanders during the Peninsular, South of France & Waterloo Campaigns of the Napoleonic Wars.

CAPTAIN BLAZE *by Elzéar Blaze*—Life in Napoleons Army.

LEJEUNE VOLUME 1 *by Louis-François Lejeune*—The Napoleonic Wars through the Experiences of an Officer on Berthier's Staff.

LEJEUNE VOLUME 2 *by Louis-François Lejeune*—The Napoleonic Wars through the Experiences of an Officer on Berthier's Staff.

CAPTAIN COIGNET *by Jean-Roch Coignet*—A Soldier of Napoleon's Imperial Guard from the Italian Campaign to Russia and Waterloo.

FUSILIER COOPER *by John S. Cooper*—Experiences in the 7th (Royal) Fusiliers During the Peninsular Campaign of the Napoleonic Wars and the American Campaign to New Orleans.

FIGHTING NAPOLEON'S EMPIRE *by Joseph Anderson*—The Campaigns of a British Infantryman in Italy, Egypt, the Peninsular & the West Indies During the Napoleonic Wars.

CHASSEUR BARRES *by Jean-Baptiste Barres*—The experiences of a French Infantryman of the Imperial Guard at Austerlitz, Jena, Eylau, Friedland, in the Peninsular, Lutzen, Bautzen, Zinnwald and Hanau during the Napoleonic Wars.

AVAILABLE ONLINE AT **www.leonaur.com**
AND FROM ALL GOOD BOOK STORES

07/09

LEONAUR

ALSO FROM LEONAUR
AVAILABLE IN SOFTCOVER OR HARDCOVER WITH DUST JACKET

CAPTAIN COIGNET *by Jean-Roch Coignet*—A Soldier of Napoleon's Imperial Guard from the Italian Campaign to Russia and Waterloo.

HUSSAR ROCCA *by Albert Jean Michel de Rocca*—A French cavalry officer's experiences of the Napoleonic Wars and his views on the Peninsular Campaigns against the Spanish, British And Guerilla Armies.

MARINES TO 95TH (RIFLES) *by Thomas Fernyhough*—The military experiences of Robert Fernyhough during the Napoleonic Wars.

LIGHT BOB *by Robert Blakeney*—The experiences of a young officer in H.M 28th & 36th regiments of the British Infantry during the Peninsular Campaign of the Napoleonic Wars 1804 - 1814.

WITH WELLINGTON'S LIGHT CAVALRY *by William Tomkinson*—The Experiences of an officer of the 16th Light Dragoons in the Peninsular and Waterloo campaigns of the Napoleonic Wars.

SERGEANT BOURGOGNE *by Adrien Bourgogne*—With Napoleon's Imperial Guard in the Russian Campaign and on the Retreat from Moscow 1812 - 13.

SURTEES OF THE 95TH (RIFLES) *by William Surtees*—A Soldier of the 95th (Rifles) in the Peninsular campaign of the Napoleonic Wars.

SWORDS OF HONOUR *by Henry Newbolt & Stanley L. Wood*—The Careers of Six Outstanding Officers from the Napoleonic Wars, the Wars for India and the American Civil War.

ENSIGN BELL IN THE PENINSULAR WAR *by George Bell*—The Experiences of a young British Soldier of the 34th Regiment 'The Cumberland Gentlemen' in the Napoleonic wars.

HUSSAR IN WINTER *by Alexander Gordon*—A British Cavalry Officer during the retreat to Corunna in the Peninsular campaign of the Napoleonic Wars.

THE COMPLEAT RIFLEMAN HARRIS *by Benjamin Harris as told to and transcribed by Captain Henry Curling, 52nd Regt. of Foot*—The adventures of a soldier of the 95th (Rifles) during the Peninsular Campaign of the Napoleonic Wars.

THE ADVENTURES OF A LIGHT DRAGOON *by George Farmer & G.R. Gleig*—A cavalryman during the Peninsular & Waterloo Campaigns, in captivity & at the siege of Bhurtpore, India.

AVAILABLE ONLINE AT www.leonaur.com
AND FROM ALL GOOD BOOK STORES

07/09

LEONAUR

ALSO FROM LEONAUR
AVAILABLE IN SOFTCOVER OR HARDCOVER WITH DUST JACKET

THE LIFE OF THE REAL BRIGADIER GERARD VOLUME 1—THE YOUNG HUSSAR 1782-1807 *by Jean-Baptiste De Marbot*—A French Cavalryman Of the Napoleonic Wars at Marengo, Austerlitz, Jena, Eylau & Friedland.

THE LIFE OF THE REAL BRIGADIER GERARD VOLUME 2—IMPERIAL AIDE-DE-CAMP 1807-1811 *by Jean-Baptiste De Marbot*—A French Cavalryman of the Napoleonic Wars at Saragossa, Landshut, Eckmuhl, Ratisbon, Aspern-Essling, Wagram, Busaco & Torres Vedras.

THE LIFE OF THE REAL BRIGADIER GERARD VOLUME 3—COLONEL OF CHASSEURS 1811-1815 *by Jean-Baptiste De Marbot*—A French Cavalryman in the retreat from Moscow, Lutzen, Bautzen, Katzbach, Leipzig, Hanau & Waterloo.

THE INDIAN WAR OF 1864 *by Eugene Ware*—The Experiences of a Young Officer of the 7th Iowa Cavalry on the Western Frontier During the Civil War.

THE MARCH OF DESTINY *by Charles E. Young & V. Devinny*—Dangers of the Trail in 1865 by Charles E. Young & The Story of a Pioneer by V. Devinny, two Accounts of Early Emigrants to Colorado.

CROSSING THE PLAINS *by William Audley Maxwell*—A First Hand Narrative of the Early Pioneer Trail to California in 1857.

CHIEF OF SCOUTS *by William F. Drannan*—A Pilot to Emigrant and Government Trains, Across the Plains of the Western Frontier.

THIRTY-ONE YEARS ON THE PLAINS AND IN THE MOUNTAINS *by William F. Drannan*—William Drannan was born to be a pioneer, hunter, trapper and wagon train guide during the momentous days of the Great American West.

THE INDIAN WARS VOLUNTEER *by William Thompson*—Recollections of the Conflict Against the Snakes, Shoshone, Bannocks, Modocs and Other Native Tribes of the American North West.

THE 4TH TENNESSEE CAVALRY *by George B. Guild*—The Services of Smith's Regiment of Confederate Cavalry by One of its Officers.

COLONEL WORTHINGTON'S SHILOH *by T. Worthington*—The Tennessee Campaign, 1862, by an Officer of the Ohio Volunteers.

FOUR YEARS IN THE SADDLE *by W. L. Curry*—The History of the First Regiment Ohio Volunteer Cavalry in the American Civil War.

AVAILABLE ONLINE AT **www.leonaur.com**
AND FROM ALL GOOD BOOK STORES
07/09

LEONAUR

ALSO FROM LEONAUR
AVAILABLE IN SOFTCOVER OR HARDCOVER WITH DUST JACKET

LIFE IN THE ARMY OF NORTHERN VIRGINIA *by Carlton McCarthy*—
The Observations of a Confederate Artilleryman of Cutshaw's Battalion During the
American Civil War 1861-1865.

HISTORY OF THE CAVALRY OF THE ARMY OF THE POTOMAC *by
Charles D. Rhodes*—Including Pope's Army of Virginia and the Cavalry Opera-
tions in West Virginia During the American Civil War.

CAMP-FIRE AND COTTON-FIELD *by Thomas W. Knox*—A New York Her-
ald Correspondent's View of the American Civil War.

SERGEANT STILLWELL *by Leander Stillwell* —The Experiences of a Union
Army Soldier of the 61st Illinois Infantry During the American Civil War.

STONEWALL'S CANNONEER *by Edward A. Moore*—Experiences with the
Rockbridge Artillery, Confederate Army of Northern Virginia, During the American
Civil War.

THE SIXTH CORPS *by George Stevens*—The Army of the Potomac, Union
Army, During the American Civil War.

THE RAILROAD RAIDERS *by William Pittenger*—An Ohio Volunteers Recollections of the Andrews Raid to Disrupt the Confederate Railroad in Georgia During the American Civil War.

CITIZEN SOLDIER *by John Beatty*—An Account of the American Civil War by a
Union Infantry Officer of Ohio Volunteers Who Became a Brigadier General.

COX: PERSONAL RECOLLECTIONS OF THE CIVIL WAR--VOLUME 1 *by
Jacob Dolson Cox*—West Virginia, Kanawha Valley, Gauley Bridge, Cotton Mountain, South Mountain, Antietam, the Morgan Raid & the East Tennessee Campaign.

COX: PERSONAL RECOLLECTIONS OF THE CIVIL WAR--VOLUME 2
by Jacob Dolson Cox—Siege of Knoxville, East Tennessee, Atlanta Campaign, the
Nashville Campaign & the North Carolina Campaign.

KERSHAW'S BRIGADE VOLUME 1 *by D. Augustus Dickert*—Manassas, Sev-
en Pines, Sharpsburg (Antietam), Fredericksburg, Chancellorsville, Gettysburg, Chick-
amauga, Chattanooga, Fort Sanders & Bean Station.

KERSHAW'S BRIGADE VOLUME 2 *by D. Augustus Dickert*—At the wilder-
ness, Cold Harbour, Petersburg, The Shenandoah Valley and Cedar Creek..

AVAILABLE ONLINE AT **www.leonaur.com**
AND FROM ALL GOOD BOOK STORES
07/09

LEONAUR

ALSO FROM LEONAUR
AVAILABLE IN SOFTCOVER OR HARDCOVER WITH DUST JACKET

THE RELUCTANT REBEL *by William G. Stevenson*—A young Kentuckian's experiences in the Confederate Infantry & Cavalry during the American Civil War..

BOOTS AND SADDLES *by Elizabeth B. Custer*—The experiences of General Custer's Wife on the Western Plains.

FANNIE BEERS' CIVIL WAR *by Fannie A. Beers*—A Confederate Lady's Experiences of Nursing During the Campaigns & Battles of the American Civil War.

LADY SALE'S AFGHANISTAN *by Florentia Sale*—An Indomitable Victorian Lady's Account of the Retreat from Kabul During the First Afghan War.

THE TWO WARS OF MRS DUBERLY *by Frances Isabella Duberly*—An Intrepid Victorian Lady's Experience of the Crimea and Indian Mutiny.

THE REBELLIOUS DUCHESS *by Paul F. S. Dermoncourt*—The Adventures of the Duchess of Berri and Her Attempt to Overthrow French Monarchy.

LADIES OF WATERLOO *by Charlotte A. Eaton, Magdalene de Lancey & Juana Smith*—The Experiences of Three Women During the Campaign of 1815: Waterloo Days by Charlotte A. Eaton, A Week at Waterloo by Magdalene de Lancey & Juana's Story by Juana Smith.

TWO YEARS BEFORE THE MAST *by Richard Henry Dana. Jr.*—The account of one young man's experiences serving on board a sailing brig—the Penelope—bound for California, between the years1834-36.

A SAILOR OF KING GEORGE *by Frederick Hoffman*—From Midshipman to Captain—Recollections of War at Sea in the Napoleonic Age 1793-1815.

LORDS OF THE SEA *by A. T. Mahan*—Great Captains of the Royal Navy During the Age of Sail.

COGGESHALL'S VOYAGES: VOLUME 1 *by George Coggeshall*—The Recollections of an American Schooner Captain.

COGGESHALL'S VOYAGES: VOLUME 2 *by George Coggeshall*—The Recollections of an American Schooner Captain.

TWILIGHT OF EMPIRE *by Sir Thomas Ussher & Sir George Cockburn*—Two accounts of Napoleon's Journeys in Exile to Elba and St. Helena: Narrative of Events by Sir Thomas Ussher & Napoleon's Last Voyage: Extract of a diary by Sir George Cockburn.

AVAILABLE ONLINE AT **www.leonaur.com**
AND FROM ALL GOOD BOOK STORES
07/09

LEONAUR

ALSO FROM LEONAUR
AVAILABLE IN SOFTCOVER OR HARDCOVER WITH DUST JACKET

ESCAPE FROM THE FRENCH *by Edward Boys*—A Young Royal Navy Midshipman's Adventures During the Napoleonic War.

THE VOYAGE OF H.M.S. PANDORA *by Edward Edwards R. N. & George Hamilton, edited by Basil Thomson*—In Pursuit of the Mutineers of the Bounty in the South Seas—1790-1791.

MEDUSA *by J. B. Henry Savigny and Alexander Correard and Charlotte-Adélaïde Dard* —Narrative of a Voyage to Senegal in 1816 & The Sufferings of the Picard Family After the Shipwreck of the Medusa.

THE SEA WAR OF 1812 VOLUME 1 *by A. T. Mahan*—A History of the Maritime Conflict.

THE SEA WAR OF 1812 VOLUME 2 *by A. T. Mahan*—A History of the Maritime Conflict.

WETHERELL OF H. M. S. HUSSAR *by John Wetherell*—The Recollections of an Ordinary Seaman of the Royal Navy During the Napoleonic Wars.

THE NAVAL BRIGADE IN NATAL *by C. R. N. Burne*—With the Guns of H. M. S. Terrible & H. M. S. Tartar during the Boer War 1899-1900.

THE VOYAGE OF H. M. S. BOUNTY *by William Bligh*—The True Story of an 18th Century Voyage of Exploration and Mutiny.

SHIPWRECK! *by William Gilly*—The Royal Navy's Disasters at Sea 1793-1849.

KING'S CUTTERS AND SMUGGLERS: 1700-1855 *by E. Keble Chatterton*—A unique period of maritime history-from the beginning of the eighteenth to the middle of the nineteenth century when British seamen risked all to smuggle valuable goods from wool to tea and spirits from and to the Continent.

CONFEDERATE BLOCKADE RUNNER *by John Wilkinson*—The Personal Recollections of an Officer of the Confederate Navy.

NAVAL BATTLES OF THE NAPOLEONIC WARS *by W. H. Fitchett*—Cape St. Vincent, the Nile, Cadiz, Copenhagen, Trafalgar & Others.

PRISONERS OF THE RED DESERT *by R. S. Gwatkin-Williams*—The Adventures of the Crew of the Tara During the First World War.

U-BOAT WAR 1914-1918 *by James B. Connolly/Karl von Schenk*—Two Contrasting Accounts from Both Sides of the Conflict at Sea D uring the Great War.

AVAILABLE ONLINE AT www.leonaur.com
AND FROM ALL GOOD BOOK STORES
07/09

LEONAUR

ALSO FROM LEONAUR
AVAILABLE IN SOFTCOVER OR HARDCOVER WITH DUST JACKET

IRON TIMES WITH THE GUARDS *by An O. E. (G. P. A. Fildes)*—The Experiences of an Officer of the Coldstream Guards on the Western Front During the First World War.

THE GREAT WAR IN THE MIDDLE EAST: 1 *by W. T. Massey*—The Desert Campaigns & How Jerusalem Was Won---two classic accounts in one volume.

THE GREAT WAR IN THE MIDDLE EAST: 2 *by W. T. Massey*—Allenby's Final Triumph.

SMITH-DORRIEN *by Horace Smith-Dorrien*—Isandlwhana to the Great War.

1914 *by Sir John French*—The Early Campaigns of the Great War by the British Commander.

GRENADIER *by E. R. M. Fryer*—The Recollections of an Officer of the Grenadier Guards throughout the Great War on the Western Front.

BATTLE, CAPTURE & ESCAPE *by George Pearson*—The Experiences of a Canadian Light Infantryman During the Great War.

DIGGERS AT WAR *by R. Hugh Knyvett & G. P. Cuttriss*—"Over There" With the Australians by R. Hugh Knyvett and Over the Top With the Third Australian Division by G. P. Cuttriss. Accounts of Australians During the Great War in the Middle East, at Gallipoli and on the Western Front.

HEAVY FIGHTING BEFORE US *by George Brenton Laurie*—The Letters of an Officer of the Royal Irish Rifles on the Western Front During the Great War.

THE CAMELIERS *by Oliver Hogue*—A Classic Account of the Australians of the Imperial Camel Corps During the First World War in the Middle East.

RED DUST *by Donald Black*—A Classic Account of Australian Light Horsemen in Palestine During the First World War.

THE LEAN, BROWN MEN *by Angus Buchanan*—Experiences in East Africa During the Great War with the 25th Royal Fusiliers—the Legion of Frontiersmen.

THE NIGERIAN REGIMENT IN EAST AFRICA *by W. D. Downes*—On Campaign During the Great War 1916-1918.

THE 'DIE-HARDS' IN SIBERIA *by John Ward*—With the Middlesex Regiment Against the Bolsheviks 1918-19.

AVAILABLE ONLINE AT **www.leonaur.com**
AND FROM ALL GOOD BOOK STORES
07/09

www.ingramcontent.com/pod-product-compliance
Lightning Source LLC
Chambersburg PA
CBHW031858090426
42741CB00005B/551

9781846778919